Musée d'Orsay

Alain Nave

Musée d'Orsay

HISTORY, ARCHITECTURE, COLLECTIONS

Translated from the French by Ellie Rea

BARNES
&NOBLE
BOOKS

Originally published
as "Le Musée d'Orsay"
by Société Nouvelle
Adam Biro,
28, rue de Sévigné,
75004 Paris.
English edition, copyright
© 1999
Société Nouvelle
Adam Biro.

*Editors, English-Language
Edition :*
Francesca Rose,
Marie-Pierre Gracedieu.
Design and Layout :
Guilhem Nave.

Printed by
Graficas Estella

ISBN 0-7607-2089-4

Printed and bound in Spain

00 01 02 03 MC 5 4 3 2 1

GRAF

Frontispiece

**Orsay
Station Clock**

(Foreground)

ANTONIN
MERCIÉ

David

1871, Bronze

Designed by
Victor Laloux, this famous
clock measuring
15 feet in diameter,
in painted and gilded
plaster, dominates
the central lobby of
the Orsay Station.
Similar to the one hanging
in the *Salle des fêtes*,
its ornamental exuberance
seems out of place
compared to the functional
purity of the glass wall
it hangs on. In the
foreground, Mercié's
David, inspired by
Florentine Renaissance
statuary, is typical
of the tastes that prevailed
from the Second Empire
to the Third Republic.
A native of Toulouse,
Mercié was twenty-seven
when he received
the Legion of Honor
for this work, an example
of which still adorns one
of the town squares
of his hometown.

English translation
by Ellie Rea

This edition
published by
Barnes & Noble, Inc.,
by arrangement with
Editions Adam Biro.

2000 Barnes & Noble Books

From Grenouillère to the Orsay Museum

Two museums stand on opposite banks of the Seine: the Louvre and the Orsay Museum. Some artists seem to hesitate between the two. Their works are shown in both the palace and the train station. Delacroix, of course, and Ingres, along with other residents of this somewhat vague period when the last flames of the Romantic and Neoclassical movements flickered dimly, and the battle for realism began. But the separation between the Louvre and Orsay is not only a

Enlightenment—"the most beautiful monuments" of human culture are exhibited there. At Orsay, a more societal perception prevailed: the contemporary point of view of the creation counts just as much as the creator. Through this staunchly multidisciplinary perspective, paintings are seen next to photographs, architecture, and decorative arts. The hierarchy of genres, styles and characteristics was abolished. Cabanel's *Venus* is exhibited together with Manet's *Olympia*.

ALBERT FLAMEN

View of a Part of the Louvre and Grenouillère from the "costé de Belle Chasse"

circa 1640 / Wash drawing
Bibliothèque nationale
de France, Paris

On the fringes of the
Marguerite de Valois Park,
the *"costé de Belle Chasse"*
is still a vacant lot.
A few homes signal
the onset of housing
development. Opposite,
across the river, where two
ship masts rise, the Louvre
and the Tuileries Gardens
stand up, with the Flore
Pavillion in the corner.
It is here, on the site
of the *"costé de Belle
Chasse"*, that
the Orsay Station
was constructed in 1900.

Preceding pages

**Façade of the
Orsay Museum
on the banks
of the Seine**

Two pavilions,
each adorned with a clock
nearly 20 feet in diameter,
frame the old departure
hall building.
Three feminine statues
top large medallions
where the letters P.O.
(Paris-Orléans)
are inscribed.
These letters recall that
the Orsay Station was also
commonly referred to as
the Orléans Station.

matter of style, it bears a date: 1848. This year was marked by a clash between political conservatism and the pragmatism of business, and by the emergence of an industrial era, leading to the rupture of social structures.

1848: realism was present both in art and in popular uprisings. These uprisings caused unrest all over Europe, from Germany to Hungary, from Poland to Italy. They brought together artists and insurgents. The French monarchy, one of old men and ministers-for-hire, was deposed for a second time. Daumier rejoiced. With a mighty hand, he painted *The Republic Nourishing its Children*. A dandy before the "exhilaration" of 1848, Baudelaire, along with a few friends founded *Le Salut Public*, illustrated with a Gustave Courbet barricade. But Louis Napoléon, proclaimed president in December, had no doubts about what the new institutions would lead to. Nevertheless, it was at this moment that common usage of the word "modern" was born.

The Meeting of Venus and Olympia

Different times, different ideas. In 1986, when the Orsay Museum was about to open, the debate was not only centered on the division of the collections. At the Louvre, the choice and presentation of the works of art were inherited by the Universalist and didactic vision of the

Actually, there are several similarities between these two works: both were painted in 1863, the year of Delacroix's death and the year when Ingres, aged eighty-four, painted his *Turkish Bath,* round, like an eye swollen with desire. *Venus* was admired and acquired by the Emperor, while *Olympia* caused a scandal. Zola said ironically: "At least if Mr. Manet had borrowed Mr. Cabanel's rice powder puff and powdered Olympia's face and breasts, the young lady would have been presentable." In one case, modern art was born, and the other was an apology of "cleanliness in painting". The spirit of Orsay can be seen in this confrontation between *Venus* and *Olympia*: the two women opened our eyes, and taught us that art is not a straight road paved with a series of recognized masterpieces. They taught us that what we see depends on what we think. Cabanel represented life for many of his contemporaries, while Manet was an oddity, as much as a Dogon statuette is for some of ours. Different times, different ideas... The differences between the Louvre and Orsay lie only in the existence of one in the eyes of the other. For example, even the architecture of Orsay is influenced by the Louvre. When Victor Laloux drew the plans for the future train station in 1897, he could not help but ponder the elegant presence of the Tuileries Gardens, the Palace's mighty facades, the Flore Pavillion, and the *Galerie du Bord de l'Eau*. This is undoubtedly one of the great ambiguities in the history of architecture. The Orsay Station was designed on the principles of a metal and glass construction. But it was dressed in stone, decorated with arcades and statues to keep it from being dwarfed by the neighboring palace. In 1900, during its inauguration, the painter Édouard Detaille pointed out this stupefying equivocation—and in quite a premonitory manner: "The train station is superb, and it looks like a palace of fine art."

It is obvious that these two havens of culture seem to share an unshakable common destiny. If we go back further in time, we discover, at the very origin of the site where the Orsay Museum now stands, the roots of this remarkable polarity between the two buildings on opposite banks of the river Seine.

Queen Margot's castle

In 1605, Marguerite de Valois, repudiated spouse of Henri IV, had lead the life of a recluse for nearly twenty years. She returned to Paris, staying at the Hôtel de Sens for a while, and had a superb palace built for her at the *Pré-aux-Clercs*, on the edge of the Left Bank, challenging the Louvre and the Tuileries. The hôtel was built and furnished between 1606 and 1609. The buildings opened onto the rue de Seine, near the *Cour Carrée* of the Louvre. The property, consisting of gardens and a park, stretched out over half a mile, running along the river all the way to what is now the rue de Bellechasse, named after an Augustinian institute founded there in 1636, in what was probably an old hunting

reserve. Today's Orsay Museum would be at the western edge of this rectangle, bordered by the rue Jacob and the rue de l'Université, its main entrance being located precisely on the rue de Bellechasse.

In her new palace, Margot dedicated herself to spiritual exercises, though never overcoming her intemperances. She attracted lovers and poets, writers and philosophers. She died in her palace on March 27, 1615. Parisians crowded around her casket, and among them were, already, her creditors. Louis XIII, her heir, agreed to sell the entire estate in 1623 in order to settle the late empress's debts.

From Faubourg Saint-Germain to the Grenouillère

Because of the location of her vast property, and its division among her many creditors, Marguerite de Valois unwillingly started the extension of the capital towards the west, where the Faubourg Saint-Germain emerged. She thus contributed to the migration of nobility and members of high society from the Right Bank towards the opposite bank where many hôtels were gradually built. The neighborhood experienced its principal expansion during the eighteenth century, when many prestigious hôtels were

FRANÇOIS CLOUET

Marguerite de Valois as a Child

circa 1560
Pencil with touches of color
Musée Condé, Chantilly.

9

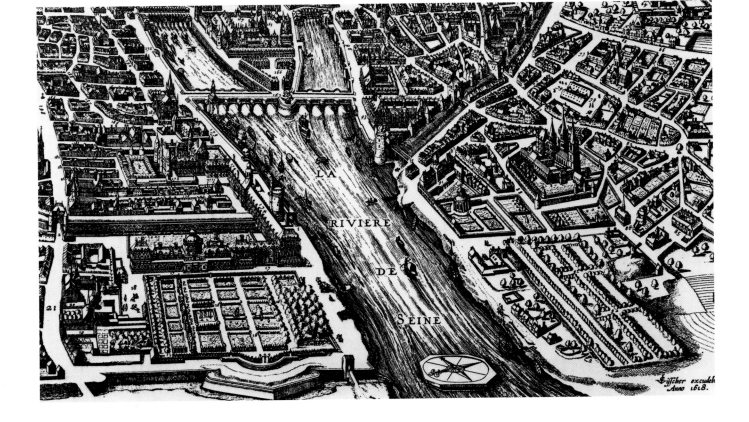

Map by Mérian

1615 (detail)

On the left bank, opposite the Tuileries of her mother, Catherine de Medicis, and the Louvre of Henri IV, her ex-husband, Marguerite de Valois built her "own space of royalty". The entrance to her palace is located on the rue de Seine. The gardens follow, in the middle of which she had a chapel built for the Augustinians (on the site of the present-day *École des beaux-arts*). Downstream, the park extends to the rue de Bellechasse. The paths which cross it served as a plan for the present-day streets.

NICOLAS DE LARGILLIÈRE

Charles Boucher d'Orsay

Oil on canvas (detail) Musée Carnavalet, Paris.

Provost of the merchants of Paris, from 1700 to 1708, he ordered the construction of a tree-lined stone quay, on the site of the so-called *Grenouillère*. Named the quai d'Orsay, it would later become quai Bonaparte in 1802,

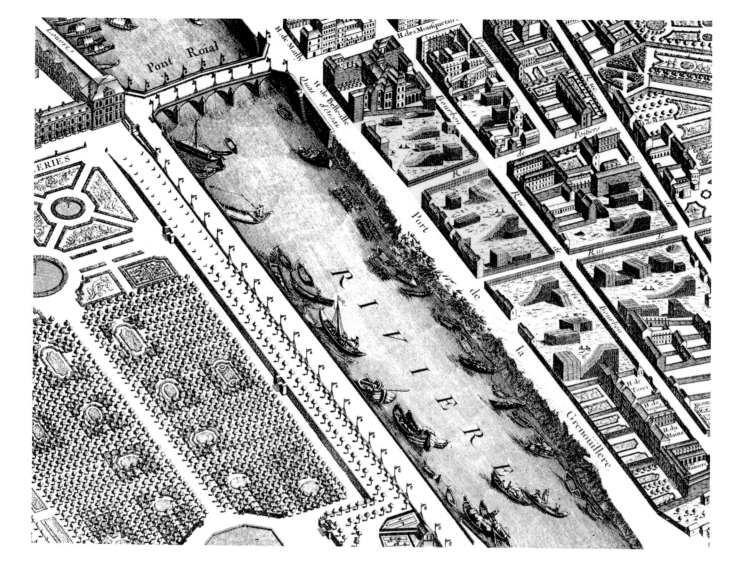

only to recover its original name in 1815. In 1983, the part that runs along the Orsay Station was renamed quai Henry-de-Montherlant.

built. Among these, one belonging to the Maréchal de Belle-Isle, still steeped in the Louis XIV style, was just a few feet from the Orsay Station. Further west was another (France's future National Assembly), belonging to the Duchess of Bourbon. Her close friend, the Marquis de Lassay, lived nearby in an hôtel whose Italianate style was highly appreciated during the Regency. Towards the end of the century, the Hôtel de Salm (transformed, in 1804, into the seat of the Legion of Honor) was built by the Prince of Salm-Kyrbourg. Located on the rue de Bellechasse, opposite the future Orsay Station, it exemplified a notable evolution in the architectural tastes of this pre-Revolutionary period. In the heart of a park, the hôtel is built according to simple architectonic principles that favor circles and squares. But for many years the land adjoining the Hôtel de Belle-Isle, on the banks of the Seine next to it, called the Grenouillère port, was occupied by large floating lumberyards, still visible on

Turgot's map of 1737-1739. The area was unfit for habitation, its cluttered grounds offensive to residents. Beginning in the early 1700s, Charles Boucher d'Orsay, the provost of merchants, undertook the development of this quay.

In 1751, a small part of the floating lumber yard was allotted to the *Coches pour la Cour* (Coaches for the Court, a company that handled the transportation of kings, princes and officers of the House of the King). This was at the site of the eastern side of the present-day station, which seems to prove a certain predisposition of this spot for transportation. After the Revolution, the coaches gave way to barracks that housed the *légion de police*, then the *garde consulaire* and various army corps.

A Palace for the Cour des comptes

In 1810, as Napoleon finished the development of the Quai de la Grenouillère, on the site of a large part of the present-day train station, he began the construction of the Orsay Palace, led by Jacques Charles Bonnard, to house the Foreign Ministry. Completed by Jacques Lacornée in 1838, the building was used for other projects, and finally given to the *Cour des comptes* (Court of Auditors) and the *Conseil d'État* (State Council).

The period was rich in public commissions and the government was keen on young talent. Delacroix decorated the Throne Room of the *Palais Bourbon* with frescoes, and later decorated the library as well. Also at the *Palais Bourbon*, Horace Vernet decorated the *Salle des pas perdus,* showing the first locomotive in French painting, *The Genius of Steam on Land* in 1838, one year after the inauguration of the first railway. This was just a few hundred yards from the future Orsay Station.

The *Cour des comptes* comissioned several young sculptors, such as Auguste Clésinger, and painters, such as Eugène

Isabey and Théodore Chassériau, to decorate the landing and grand staircase. But after some thirty years of existence, the building was set ablaze on May 24, 1871, during the throes of the Commune. None of the ruins were saved, except for a few relics—notably some frescoes by Chassériau, today on display at the Louvre.

After this period of turmoil, the young Republic exhumed its buildings from the rubble. No decision was made concerning the ruins of the Orsay Palace, set between those of the Hôtel Salm—restored in 1878—and the old Hôtel de Belle-Isle—rebuilt in 1890 for the *Caisse des Dépôts et Consignations* (The Deposit and Consignment Office). Should they revive the old *Cour des comptes?* Build new administrative buildings? At one point, the idea of building a decorative arts museum was considered. The project was approved, and, in 1880, Rodin was commissioned to create a monumental door illustrating Dante's *Divine Comedy.* The original plaster of *The Gates of Hell,* in which *Adam, Eve* and *The Thinker* are present, can be found today in its rightful place, at the Orsay Museum. It seemed as though the authorities were taking their time in deciding, but there were more than sixty other projects proposed. Finally, in 1896, the State sold the land to the *Compagnie des*

chemins de fer d'Orléans (the Orléans Railroad Company). An agreement was signed on April 2, 1897, which freed the area around the ruins of the Orsay Palace, including the site of the old barracks adjoining it and the part of the rue de Poitiers that separated them.

This land was sold for 10,500,000 French Francs. The aim was to establish a new railway terminus in the heart of Paris, so that travelers on their way to Orléans or the southwest would not have to get their trains at the Austerlitz Station, which was thought to be too far from the center of the city. Planned for the inauguration of the World Exhibition of 1900, the new station assured its connection to Austerlitz thanks to an underground two-rail line about 2.5 miles long

that ran along the Left Bank quays—the same infrastructure that the RER commuter trains use today.

The Construction of the Orsay Station

After purchasing the land, the Orléans Company held a competition among three renowned architects: Émile Bénard, Lucien Magne, and Victor Laloux. Three options were studied: a station without hotel facilities, a station with a simple hotel, or a station with a luxury hotel.

Another constraint was added to the company's requirements—the building had to have two facades: the main one for departures, facing the quay on the Seine, the other for arrivals, on the rue de Bellechasse, facing the Hôtel de Salm.

A designated committee selected Laloux's project, and ratified the decision on April 21, 1898. As Jean Jenger recalled in *Orsay: From Station to Museum,* the architect's design was based on a few major ideas. "In front of the Tuileries, not far from the Louvre on the banks of the Seine, in one of the most elegant corners of Paris, [the building] must satisfy both the requirements of a modern train station

11

and the architectural surroundings that impose on it a monumental and decorative appearance. These principles moved us to exclude, from the very beginning, the more obvious idea of building it in iron. Only stone shall be visible in the future station, only stone could replace the *Cour des comptes* and face the Tuileries."

A Haven of Pleasure!

The project for a luxury hotel was adopted. It spread out on the rue de Bellechasse facade, above the arrivals entrance, continuing, six floors high, in the corner building on the Seine side and all along the rue de Lille —one of the old paths of Queen Margot's park. Its 370 rooms boasted the comfort that a hotel for travelers demanded. The establishment was so elegant that its lounges quickly became havens of pleasure. In 1926, Thomas Mann recalled, "It is a place where the bourgeoisie in Paris celebrates —the choice location for wedding receptions, association balls and other annoying ceremonies. There is at least one here every day. On the various floors, waiters in morning coats, chains around their necks, greet you and lead you in. Young people flirt on the stairs, and the music is appalling."

The reception hall—located on the Seine side above the station cafeteria—boasted a neo-rocaille decor of gilded stucco frieze columns and pilasters, fluted in parts. It was covered with an abundance of cornices decorated with indolent cherubs. Mirrors amplified the electric glare of the lighting and the sparkle of the crystal chandeliers. On the ceiling was *Apollo's Chariot Surrounded by Springtime Figures*, a vast composition by Pierre Fritel, whose studio probably made the arches and medallions.

Nearby, on the Bellechasse facade, was the famous Dining Room—about 100 feet long—decorated with Gabriel Ferrier's *Allegory of the Periods of Time*, magnificently restored to its original decor of stucco, mirrors and gold. Laloux also put in a few small reception rooms on this level. The Louis XV Room, designed for intimate receptions, was

Seine Façade of the Orsay Station in construction

Photograph,
September 1899
Private collection.

In May 1899,
the foundations were completed.
The construction of the station began.
Visible in this photograph,
which shows the arcade of the eastern pavilion
in the foreground,
is the facing of the
Charente and Poitou stone façade on the metallic framework.

invariably furnished in the rocaille style. The Reading Room, embellished with a ceiling by Benjamin-Constant in pink and gray tones and bearing the enigmatic title, *The Routes of Air*, in which Victoire and a thunderbolt-bearing knight face off. There was also a Smoking Room, whose walls were covered with wood paneling, and tapestries.

"Monumental and decorative"

The Orsay Station was a technical and architectural masterpiece, a huge inverted vessel, a gigantic metallic framework dressed in stone: the structure alone was made up of 12,000 tons of metal, almost double that of the Eiffel Tower. The lobby of the station consisted of a vaulted central nave—450 feet long, 105 feet high, and a span of 130 feet—which supported an immense glass roof sheltering fifteen tracks, laid below the quay, on which two hundred trains transited daily. The central nave was bordered, on the Seine side, by a narrower nave topped with seven elliptical domes. Decorated by two Fernand Cormon paintings, *Biarritz* and *Amboise*, this departure hall led to the quay through seven monumental arches. At the two ends of the central nave were large vertical glass walls, the one on the Bellechasse side with the famous clock with the gilded staff designed by Laloux. One of the great novelties of the railway building was the suppression of noise thanks to the use, for the first time in France, of electric locomotives that the travelers fondly nicknamed "saltboxes", because of their shape. This novelty allowed the architects to deal with volume in a new way. Victor Laloux wrote, "With the disappearance of steam, large station halls will naturally have to take on the appearance of large lobbies decorated in a more comfortable and luxurious manner." So he hid the metal framework of the building in the interior of his station. Covering it with sculpted and painted staff casings, he made it look like a Roman basilica, a style quite common in public buildings—especially religious ones—that had become popular again since the end of the eighteenth century.

On the exterior, the facade along the Seine was the most remarkable, with its two pavilions, both with arches. Shielded by slate roofs, the two pavilions were decorated with stone obelisks, and large clocks, measuring twenty feet in diameter, were built into their pediments. Between the two pavilions, the facade had seven glass arches decorated with a frieze, and there were three colossal feminine statues, allegorical representations of the three large cities served by the railway: *Bordeaux*, by Jean-Baptiste Hughes, *Toulouse*, by Laurent Marqueste, and *Nantes*, by Jean-Antoine Injalbert, city to which the sculptor gave the features of Mrs. Victor Laloux. On the rue de Bellechasse side, where the facade was punctuated by cornices, medallions and garlands, nine bay windows above the huge glass canopy bathed the hotel's dining room in light. On the rue de Lille side, occupied solely by the hotel, the decor was more somber and functional.

"Monumental and decorative", to quote Victor Laloux's expression, the train station was built in record time. Designed in early 1897, the project was approved in April 1898. The destruction of the barracks and the vestiges of the *Cour des comptes* began at the same time, while tracks were laid between the Austerlitz and Orsay stations. The foundation of the station was completed in May 1899. The Orsay Station was inaugurated on July 14, 1900, and was a total success. The architectural quality of the building was emulated even in the United States: it inspired the great train stations in Washington, D.C. and New York City.

From Train Station to Museum

The development of the capital and the diversification of individual and collective means of transportation—the first Metro line was opened in 1900—soon made apparent the contradictions between the two train stations on the same line. After much procrastination, a decision was made in 1935, choosing the Austerlitz station as the main train station for the major lines, reducing Orsay to a station for suburban lines. For some time, the immense nave only appeared as an antediluvian novelty that many already thought of remodeling for other purposes. Only a few events prove that it continued to exist. In 1945, the Orsay Station accommodated prisoners of war and deportees returning from Germany. In May 1958, General De Gaulle held a conference at the hotel to announce his return to political life. Orson Welles used it, in 1962, as a set for his film adaptation of Kafka's *The Trial*. In 1973, Madeleine Renaud and Jean-Louis Barrault's theatrical company set up shop there. Also in 1973, the hotel ceased activity. The next year, for some time, the station housed the Drouot collections. During this period, the train station was rented out for conferences and symposiums, while the reduced railroad activities withdrew to the basement, and progressively faded out completely towards the end of the 1960s. In fact, the decision to sell Orsay and demolish it had been made already in 1961. A competition was launched to develop a space dedicated to an international hotel complex. It attracted some of the most famous architects of the time, such as Le Corbusier, for whom the site would serve as the "possible onset of the future volumetric analysis of Paris." At the end of the competition, an 820-room hotel, a swimming pool, a shopping mall and several restaurants were planned. In 1971, when all of the permits seemed to have been granted, Jacques Duchamel, Minister of Cultural Affairs,

vetoed the plan with strong support from President Georges Pompidou. Two years later, an idea was developed to create a "transition museum between the Louvre and Beaubourg"—the latter was still in construction at that time—to assemble the artistic movements of the Second Empire and the Third Republic. On October 20, 1977, the new president, Valéry Giscard d'Estaing, called a restricted ministerial council that made an irrevocable decision. Partially listed in the supplementary Register of Historical Monuments in 1973, when the public was shocked by the destruction of the Baltard markets, the Orsay Station and hotel were permanently registered in March 1978. On June 5, 1979, the President and Jean-Philippe Lecat, Minister of Culture, selected the project of an agency named ACT Architecture, designed by Pierre Colboc, Renaud Bardon and Jean-Paul Philippon. In 1980, the Italian architect Gae Aulenti was asked to handle the museum's interior design. Demolition and infrastructure work began in 1981, and construction reached cruising speed in the summer of 1983.

The work concerned the rehabilitation of the group of buildings and the reorientation of the principal facade on the rue de Bellechasse. Restoration of the decor began, for the hotel lounges and the train station, repairing the staff caissons on the vaults and the archivolts, where ventilation inlets and acoustic devices were placed. The great central nave became a key central space, and the museum structures were built in its sides, while the domed rooms in the lobby were refurbished. Finally, the surface and spaces were livened up, and the works of art presented.

The collections covering the years 1848 to 1870 were distributed throughout the ground floor: these were works of Realism and the beginnings of Impressionism, as well as Romanticism, Eclecticism, and Orientalism. Sculpture and decorative arts up to the beginning of the Third Republic were also displayed there, along with architectural models and designs, notably those of the Paris Opera.

On the intermediate level, the collections covering the years 1870 to 1910 were presented: the art and decorations of the Third Republic, the Naturalist, Symbolist, and Academic movements, as well as Art Nouveau. Works of the Impressionist period and all the Post-Impressionist schools were exhibited on the second floor, under the glass wall and loft of the lobby.

On December 9, 1986, the museum opened its doors to the public. "A place of conflict among innovation and tradition, technology and fine art, engineers and architects," as Michel Ragon said. At that time, the Orsay Museum exhibited about three thousand works of art for the pleasure of the nine thousand visitors welcomed daily into Victor Laloux's nave.

13

HENRI
ROYER

**Portrait
of Victor Laloux**

Drawing (detail)

Winner of the Prix
de Rome in 1878,
Victor Laloux (1850-
1937), architect
of the Orsay Station,
was already famous for
the construction of several
buildings in Tours,
his hometown: the Saint
Martin basilica, the train
station and the City Hall.
Several public buildings
in Roubaix can be
attributed to him,
as well as the completion
of the *Crédit Lyonnais* bank
headquarters in Paris,
from 1907 to 1913.

From Queen Margot to the Orsay Palace

ANONYMOUS

"The Great Design" of Henri IV circa 1603

Galerie des Cerfs / Château de Fontainebleau

This mural represents "the Great Design" of Henri IV, destined to remodel the Louvre and the Tuileries Gardens. The vast project was never successfully completed, only the *Galerie du Bord de l'Eau* connecting the two palaces was constructed. The piece reveals the absence of urbanization at the time along the opposite bank of the Seine, in this area bordered by swamps, called the *Pré-aux-Clercs*. On the left, a path (the present-day rue du Bac?) seems to lead up to the *Saint-Germain (des Prés)* abbey. Marguerite de Valois purchased the land, at that time property of the University, where she built her estate, starting in 1606. The location of the future Orsay Station is near the last building, on the top right.

FRANÇOIS-ÉTIENNE VILLERET

The quai d'Orsay in 1839

1839 / Watercolor, pen, ink and gouache / Musée Carnavalet, Paris.

Begun under the Empire, completed in 1838, the Orsay Palace, before being assigned to the *Cour des comptes* and *Conseil d'État*, was intended for the accommodation of visiting ambassadors. As historian Jean-Marc Leri remarked, the emperor wished to see, from the Tuileries, "the crowd of ambassadors paying homage to him through his minister." Thus, the new palace was to be the symbol of France's influence on Europe and the entire world. To the right of the palace, in the shadows, is the Hôtel de Salm built in 1786, which Napoléon transformed into the seat of the Legion of Honor. Behind the Orsay Palace, the barracks separated from it by the rue de Poitiers: the palace (destroyed by fire in 1871), the barracks and the street constituted the site of the future train station. Opposite the Louvre and Tuileries, the quay, built almost thirty years before, was a popular Parisian promenade.

The Orsay Station

**Construction
of the Orsay Station:
The departure
lobby**

January 1900
Photograph
Fonds Urphot,
Orsay Museum, Paris.

The project by
the architect Laloux was
accepted in April 1898.
The buildings began to rise
in the middle of 1899.
Visible here are the elliptic
domes of the departure
lobby, on the Seine side,
which borders
the central nave, topped
with the great loft.
With the use of 12 tons
of metallic structure,
engineers were as much
involved in the
construction
of the Orsay Station
as the architect, as there
were numerous problems
arising from
such an enterprise.

17

**Interior view
of the Orsay Station**

circa 1910 / Photograph
Fonds Urphot,
Orsay Museum, Paris.

Originally the Orsay
Station was conceived
as the railway terminus,
in the heart of the capital,
of the Orléans-Southwest
network, at that time
served by the
Austerlitz Station, which
was thought to be too
far away for Parisians.
For the first time,
a luxuriant dressing for
the metallic skeleton
was made possible thanks
to the suppression of noise
pollution by the use
of electric locomotives.
Here, the departure lobby:
Laloux decorated its ends
with paintings by
Fernand Cormon, *Biarritz*
and *Amboise.*

**Exterior view
of the Orsay Station**

circa 1900 / Photograph

On July 14, 1900,
after eighteen months
of work, the train station
was inaugurated for the
International Exhibition.
Responding to the wishes
of its sponsors, who gave
priority to the appearance
of the building, Laloux
concealed the "railroad"
allure of the station
in order to integrate
it into an architecturally
sensitive neighborhood.

**Interior view
of the Orsay Station**

circa 1900 / Photograph

Without a veritable
solution concerning
the continuity of the
exterior façades,
the treatment of the
interior is closer
to Roman architecture
than that of a railroad
hall—which led Laloux's
contemporaries to joke
ironically about his
Diocletian mania.
Faithful to the esthetics
of his time, mindful
of the possibilities
awakened by the spread
of electricity, notably with
the use of the "saltboxes"
(the first electric
locomotives put
to use in France),
the Orsay Station also
exemplified remarkable
technological feats:
300,000 sq. ft. of flooring,
1,200,000 sq. ft.
of framework,
400,000 sq. ft. of glass,
12,000 ft. of tracks...
to serve 200 trains
each day.

The Orsay Museum

**Transforming
the train station
into a museum**

Above
Photograph,
November 13, 1981

The beginning
of the demolition
and the rehabilitation
of the structure.

Below
Photograph,
September 11, 1985

The construction
of the central nave with
the placing of the staff
casings on the vaults
and the erection
of the museum structures.

Beginning in the 1930s,
the Orsay Station was just
a suburban line terminal.
Thirty years later, the train
station nearly disappeared
in favor of a commercial
and hotel complex.
The trauma caused by the
destruction of the Baltard
markets, and a renewed
interest in "fine arts"
architecture, salvaged
Laloux's masterpiece. In
1973, Georges Pompidou
accepted the idea to turn it
into "a transition museum
between the Louvre
and Beaubourg". In 1977,
President Valéry Giscard
d'Estaing ratified this
choice. Guided by a
project proposed by the
ACT Architecture agency,
work began in 1981.
The museum opened
to the public
on December 9, 1986.

Orsay Museum: the Bellechasse façade

The rehabilitation of the train station reached the exterior of the building as well, notably with the repair of the glass canopies and the reorientation, on the rue de Bellechasse side, of the principal façade. Placed in front of the museum are three of the four cast-iron animal statues that served as decorations at the 1878 International Exhibition: *Horse with Harrow,* by Rouillard, *Young Elephant Caught in a Trap,* by Fremiet, and *Rhinoceros* by Jacquemart, while *Taurus,* by Cain, remained in Nîmes. To the right, on the rue de Lille side, the statues symbolizing the six continents, which were also displayed at Trocadéro for the International Exhibition of 1878, were installed.

Facing page

Orsay Museum: the central nave

The central nave, 105 feet high, is the heart of the organization of the museum. One year after accepting ACT Architecture's project, the interior design of the museum was entrusted to Gae Aulenti. The architect's wish was not to imitate Laloux's choices, but to use form to compose lines whose rigor would preserve the expression of the original architecture and that of the works of art being exhibited. In the foreground, the original plaster of the *Four Corners of the World* by Carpeaux magnifies the movement of figures that accompanies the rotation of the celestial sphere.

The Salle des fêtes

Designed by Laloux, in a gold stucco neo-rocaille decor, this room's ceiling is decorated with *Apollo's Chariot* by Pierre Fritel. Splendidly restored and placed on the Orsay Museum collection visitor route, this space is a veritable celebration room of the official art of the Third Republic.

In this setting, representative of the dominant eclecticism and apotheosis of Salon art, are exhibited the prized works of republican councilors and notabilities. Sculptures include the pirouetting *Warrior Dance* by Segoffin, *Nature Revealing Herself to Science*, by Barrias, which combines marble, onyx, malachite and lapis-lazuli, and *The Aurora* in white and pink marble by Denys Puech in which the fluidity of the woman's hair stands out against the severe sensuality of her body. Paintings include war-inspired works by Alphonse de Neuville and allegoric paintings by Lefebvre. Nothing is missing, right up to mythological painting by Bouguereau whose *The Birth of Venus* evokes the memory of Ingres and Raphaël, in an attempt to forget Cabanel's *Birth*.

The Dining Room

The Dining Room, around 100 feet long, is another room that the Orsay Museum
restored to its original brilliance and reassigned to its initial activity: delicacies.
Here, a mix of stucco, glass and gold dominates. On the immense ceiling,
Allegory of the Periods of Time, an ethereal composition by Gabriel Ferrier, unfolds in all its splendor
on three panels. Even the overdoors are punctuated by echoes of this bluish symphony.

The Orsay Museum
Collections

ANONYMOUS

The Luxembourg Museum

Late 19th century
Drawing
Bibliothèque des Arts
décoratifs, Paris.

Preceding pages

EDGAR DEGAS

Young 14 Year-old Dancer

1881 / Bronze, tulle, satin
The sculpture is
surrounded by four
dancers and a horse
(wax statuettes offered
by the American collector
Paul Mellon).

"They are exercises to get
me started, nothing more."
Degas, who took up
sculpture in 1881 working
with wax and clay, always
remained in the back-
ground of this means of
expression. Except for *La
Petite Danseuse* presented
at the 1881 exhibition,
he refused to show his statuettes. Upon his death, one
hundred fifty of them were
discovered at his studio, of
which only one half were
saved and cast in bronze.

"Like long echoes lost in the distance [...] odors, colors and sounds call to each other." Half a century later Marcel Proust replied to these verses by Baudelaire: "All that which shares the same time looks alike."

In the treasures of its collections, which include all the artistic activities between the generations of Baudelaire and Proust, the Orsay Museum possesses the distinctive feature of confronting works of art of diverse origin and function, and of different periods. Sculpture, drawing and painting "call to each other", but so do the other visual arts: photography, invented by Daguerre in 1839—the museum holds about 13,000 negatives—and the cinematograph of the Lumière brothers, which appeared in 1895 and was preceded by brilliant "coelacanths" like Muybridge, Marey, and Reynaud.

This was also a century during which art established a link with industry—the first "Great Exposition of the Works of Industry of All Nations" opened to the public at London's Crystal Palace in 1851. The decorative or applied arts are therefore well presented at Orsay. These are everyday objects, whose material and plastic form required the undivided attention of both artist and artisan: goldsmith, glassblower, furniture maker, potter, metalworker. They range from works of the Second Empire up to the sinuous forms of Art Nouveau and its many international variations.

Finally, to complete the fields of visual creativity, the Orsay Museum is also particularly devoted to architecture, in the form of drawings: those of Labrouste, Viollet-le-Duc, Baltard and Garnier, but also models like the exceptional 1:100 scale reconstruction of the Opera quarter, as it appeared in 1914.

The Composition of the Collections

Not counting the thousands of prints contained in the photographic collections, the Orsay Museum contains about 6,000 works of art. Half of these are part of permanent exhibits, which represent some 1,100 paintings, 700 sculptures and 800 objets d'art. Although the museum had to make significant purchases, in order to respond to the concepts of museology on which the Orsay project is based, these works of art were obviously not all acquired after the museum was established.

To a great extent, especially concerning paintings, its collections have a common origin with those of the Louvre. They date back to the birth of the Royal Gallery of the Luxembourg Museum, in 1818.

From the Luxembourg Museum to the Louvre

The Luxembourg Museum, created by Louis XVIII, was dedicated to the presentation of works by contemporary artists, that had been purchased by the State. "The most beautiful specimens" reached the summit of the Louvre ten years after the death of their creators. Originally set up in a wing at the seat of the Senate, the museum was moved to the *Orangerie,* established by the architect Gisors, in 1886, to which was added the room that opens onto the rue de Vaugirard.

The enrichment of the Luxembourg collections depended primarily on the purchase of works exhibited at the Salon, a periodic event that began in 1667, organized at the Louvre in the Salon Carré—whence its name. But the panel of judges, not very moved by innovative audacity, long preferred styles that flirted with official esthetics—even Delacroix learned this at his expense.

Shortly after the Commune, this state of mind changed. Public taste shifted toward the Realist school and the Barbizon painters; so much so, that at the end of the 1870s the Fine Arts Administration came forward during the sales of the studio collections of Millet, Diaz and Daubigny, some time after their deaths.

The art market gave a remarkable reception to the works of these artists. In 1881, Millet's *Angelus* was sold for 160,000 French Francs; it had been purchased from the painter for 1,000 French Francs when the painting was completed in 1859. In 1890, it was bought back by Alfred Chauchard for a total of 800,000 French francs, a considerable sum that reminds us how in thirty years the work had become so popular, as venerated as the *Mona Lisa* is today.

Another event in 1881 confirmed the infatuation for the schools: Juliette Courbet, the sister of the artist, gave the Louvre *Burial at Ornans*. Not only did this act evince the permeability between the Louvre and the Luxembourg Museum, it also attested to the recognition of public administrators for the artist, four years after his death in exile. This gift also demonstrated how often the collections of the State were open to the generosity of certain families—which was the case, later, for Fantin-Latour, Pissarro, Renoir, Luce, Signac, Redon and many others. Finally, this period saw the beginnings of an increased generosity of collectors, who helped add to the quantity and variety of works, and who were more hostile to the creamy beauty of the pompier-style nymphs than the councilors of the Third Republic were. These gestures of generosity spread following the initiatives of rich bourgeois like Madame Boucicaut—the wife of the founder of the Bon Marché store—who, in 1888, parted with Fromentin's *Egyptian Women on the Banks of the Nile*. That same year, Madame Pommery purchased Millet's *The Gleaners,* donating it two years later. "It is a nationalist and patriotic thing that I wanted to do by giving this masterpiece to the Louvre," she told the mayor of Reims.

But virtuous selflessness is not always appreciated for its true worth, judging by the scandal provoked by Manet's *Olympia*. Already protected by two guards during the 1865 Salon, its entry into the Luxembourg Museum in 1890—thanks to the tenacity of a few irreducible benefactors led by Monet—took place amidst booing.

The Caillebotte "affair" gave rise to an identical scandal. In 1894, upon the death of the painter, an unfailing supporter of the Impressionists, his collection was bequeathed to the State. It was an admirable collection, containing only masterpieces: Manet's *The Balcony*; Monet's *The Saint-Lazare Station*; Renoir's *Bal du Moulin de la Galette*; Cézanne's *L'Estaque*.

During the negotiations with the Administration, his brother added two paintings by Caillebotte himself to these marvels, one of which was *The Floor Scrapers*. But the Administration accepted only 38 of the 67 works in the bequest. Half of the Monets were rejected, along with one-third of the Sisleys and three-quarters of the Pissarros. In 1897, the collection was finally exhibited in an annex of the Luxembourg Museum. A general outcry ensued. The following was written in the *Journal des artistes:* "It is an ugly and shameful lair." Gérôme, one of the period's great painters, went even further: "Those people paint beneath themselves." This level of conservatism can seem appalling to us now. The same year, in Barcelona, young Picasso, in a style resembling some "terrible Forain paintings", as Apollinaire referred to it, was already famous.

In 1895, one year after the death of Gustave Caillebotte, another bequest was made. It placated the public's enthusiasm for French painting of the years 1830-1850. It was the Barbizon collection, which, by its age, deserved to go directly to the Louvre. In his will, the businessman Georges Thomy-Thiéry left 121 paintings (12 Corots, 11 Delacroix, some paintings by Millet, Daubigny, Rousseau and Dupré) as well as 147 Barye sculptures—almost his entire life's work. Gustave Caillebotte's Impressionist stunt in the heart of the institution and the victory of Thomy-Thiéry's Barbizon Pre-Impressionists were a prelude to the Moreau-Nélaton donation, in 1906, composed of more than one hundred paintings that bridged the gap between these two schools.

A painter and art historian, Moreau-Nélaton owned a collection that his grandfather, a friend of Delacroix, began, his father continued, and that he himself continually added to. First presented to the State in 1907, it was enriched by a second donation in 1919, and then the 1927 bequest. Like Caillebotte's collection, the Étienne Moreau-Nélaton collection showed remarkably confident taste, encompassing entire areas of nineteenth-century painting. Delacroix, Chassériau, Daumier and Corot were present with some major works, just as the Impressionists and their precursors: Manet with *Le Déjeuner sur l'herbe*—a manifesto of modern art, painted in 1863—as well as Sisley and Monet, notably his *Poppies*, from the Argenteuil period. The collection is rich in well-loved painters, like Fantin-Latour, with *Hommage à Delacroix* —which demonstrated the admiration of the new school for

Preceding page, right

FRENCH SCHOOL

View of a Room at the Luxembourg Museum

1880 / Oil on canvas
Louvre Museum, Paris.

27

GUSTAVE CAILLEBOTTE

Self-portrait

1892 / Oil on canvas

"At Argenteuil, I also met the painter Caillebotte, the first 'protector' of the Impressionists. No hint of speculation in the purchases he made from us; he just wanted to help some friends. It was quite simple actually: he only bought things that were reputed to be unsaleable."
Auguste Renoir

the master's flamboyancy— and his friend Eugène Carrière, Puvis de Chavannes, Maillol and others.

Alfred Chauchard, founder of the *Grands Magasins du Louvre*—the company that took over the management of the hotel at the Orsay Station in 1900—completed what already looked like a nice anthology of nineteenth-century painting in 1909. Admirer of the Barbizon School, Chauchard, who Goncourt's malicious *Journal* described as "a petty parvenu who only opens his hand for that which brings publicity to his vanity" bequeathed—vanity aside—works by Rousseau, Dupré, Daubigny, Diaz, Millet's famous *Angelus*, and some splendid Corots. Moreover, the industrialist's treasures contained works by Eugène Isabey and Delacroix, including *The Tiger Hunt*, as well as one of the great icons of Napoleonic mythology, the celebrated *French Campain* by Meissonier.

To crown this extravagant collection, an even more prestigious bequest was made in 1911 by Count Isaac de Camondo, banker and impassioned art lover. As Pierre Assouline reported in his book dedicated to the family's dynasty, the Count declared, "I am not French in the legal sense of the word, that is understood. [...] But can I do something more French than leave all of my collections (all of them) to France for the Louvre museum? [...] Everything in there is for France, everything!"

On June 4, 1914, as Europe was on the brink of catastrophe, the collection was exhibited in seven rooms on the second floor of the Louvre. That day, Apollinaire wrote, "Ingres, Delacroix, Barye, Millet, Daumier, Corot and Puvis de Chavannes are well-represented here. But here is Manet's *The Fifer* and his 'pink and black jewel', *Lola de Valence,* flower of evil celebrated by Baudelaire. Above all, here are the Cézannes, *The Suicide's House*, and *The Blue Vase*. Here are the Jongkinds. Here are the Toulouse-Lautrecs, a real triumph; here are some works by Renoir, who, one day, will be better represented at the Louvre; finally here are the Degas. Now, the Luxembourg Museum just needs to get a move on, may it change sites quickly and modernize, may it not fear the avant-garde schools, may it be Orphist, Simultaneist, Futurist, Cubist, because here it is already late and the real modern art museum in Paris is now the Louvre."

Carried away by his enthusiasm, the poet forgot to add the works by Delacroix, Boudin, Pissarro and Sisley, as well as some essential Monets to his inventory. Nor should we ever forget the arrival, during the dark years of the war, of the Auguste Rodin donation that included the original plaster casts of *Balzac*, *Ugolin*, and *The Gates of Hell*.

Some time after the return to peace, the Luxembourg Museum was reorganized, but it did not give up its role as a museum for living artists. In 1922, the international schools were all moved to the *Jeu de Paume*—this museum already exhibited some masterpieces, such as Whistler's *Arrangement in Black and Grey No. 1: The Artist's Mother*. The Impressionist collections, which constituted, in some manner, the epoch's "historical avant-garde", were returned to the Louvre beginning in 1929. Between the two wars, interest for the Impressionist and Post-Impressionist schools became more generalized, to the detriment of the academic art of "our dear masters." The enrichment of the collections continued, but the purchases turned out to be financially over-cautious, and were fortunately supported by donators. Painting remained the area of predilection, and the decorative arts were long neglected, suffering from the discredit that affected the productions of Art Nouveau.

Among the donors were Joseph Reinach, Ernest May, John Quinn, Ambroise Vollard and Auguste Pellerin—gentlemen who marked the 1920s—with donations of works by Monet, Pissarro, Sisley, many Cézannes, Seurat's *Cirque* and Gauguin's *La Belle Angèle.* Other equally sumptuous gifts marked the next decade. Bequests by Koechlin, and Jacques Doucet, the latter with its enigmatic *Snake Charmer* by Douanier Rousseau, and the bequest of Antonin Personnaz in 1937, containing such seminal Impressionist works as Monet's *The Bridge at Argenteuil* and *Bust of a Young Woman Nude*, some works by Pissarro, Guillaumin, Renoir, Berthe Morisot, Degas, Sysley, Mary Cassatt, and Toulouse-Lautrec's *Jane Avril Dancing*.

Between the Jeu de Paume *and the Museum of Modern Art*

Other than the Personnaz donation, another event occurred during the artistic year of 1937: it became evident that the Luxembourg Museum had become too small. So, it was abandoned in favor of the new National Museum of Modern Art, set up in a wing of the *Palais de Tokyo,* whose name comes from the quay it overhangs, that had been built for the International Exhibition. The building was inaugurated with a retrospective of French art. Henri Focillon, with accents that Malraux would recall, wrote in the catalog, "The great architects of mural figures help Gauguin build a statue of ancient man in brilliant and mute harmony, in the Canary Islands, and, in front of Sainte-Baume and Sainte-Victoire, Cézanne dreams of Poussin. But they were all seeking examples, not models; they were out

ANONYMOUS

Portrait of Étienne Moreau-Nélaton

Photograph

BENJAMIN-CONSTANT

Portrait of Alfred Chauchard

1896 / Oil on canvas

to discover their own secrets. They have multiplied the resources of art." But this humanist was not able to stir up the new storm alone. Beginning in 1939, most of the museum's masterpieces were put in safe places. The *Jeu de Paume* was used as a deposit for art works seized by the occupying Nazis, before they were transported to Germany.

After the Liberation, a reorganization was necessary for the return of these works. In 1947, since the Louvre was full, the galleries of the *Jeu de Paume* were converted to house the Impressionist and Post-Impressionist schools. Also in 1947, the National Museum of Modern Art experienced its true beginnings, thanks to the activities of its director Jean Cassou. This museum consequently housed the new "historical avant-garde" works—Neo-Impressionists, Nabis, Fauvists, Cubists, etc.— which initiated visitors into contemporary creations.

During this period, which ran from the post-war years up to the project for the Orsay Museum, acquisitions continued either directly through purchases, through donations and bequests, or through endowments, from 1968 on, as payment of inheritance taxes.

It is important to remember that, among the major contributions from 1949 to 1958, were the various donations by the children of the famous Doctor Gachet who hosted Cézanne and Van Gogh at Auvers-sur-Oise. In addition to the many paintings by these two painters, works of Guillaumin, Monet, Pissarro and Renoir were given. One must not forget the donation of landscape paintings made by Eduardo Mollard in 1961, or that of the art dealer Max Kaganovitch, who, in 1973, offered twenty paintings, including works by Monet, Cézanne, Van Gogh and Gauguin, that had the important merit of showing the transition between Impressionism and Fauvism.

Finally, the Orsay Museum!

The division of the art works was planned starting in 1978, at the beginning of the preparatory phase of the Orsay project. The collection was broken down as follows: all of the schools from the end of Romanticism on left the Louvre. The entire contents of the *Jeu de Paume* were transferred. Finally, all of the collections prior to 1905 were removed from the National Museum of Modern Art—later works had been moved to the Centre Georges-Pompidou, which had opened its doors in 1977.

These various sources were not, however, sufficient. An extensive purchasing policy became necessary. It was important to maintain the coherence of certain schools, such as Symbolism, and balance some areas, including Neo-Impressionism, which saw the arrival of works by Seurat, Signac and Van Rysselberghe, or the Nabis and the Pont-Aven school. Some glaring gaps also needed to be filled, notably the international collections: there was only one painting each by

Munch and Klimt at Orsay, recently purchased works whose presence proved themselves indispensable.

In only a few years, through purchases, deposits, donations and endowments, some remarkable works of art came to augment the collection. These were the thirty-six *Busts of Members of Parliament* by Daumier, in unbaked colored clay, due to the generosity of David Weill. There was Courbet's *Origin of the World*, from the collection of psychoanalyst Jacques Lacan, *The Proud rue Montorgueil* by Monet, *Nude Dressing* by Degas, Gauguin's *Yellow Christ*, Van Gogh's *Starry Night*, and several Bonnards obtained during the years 1970-1980.

These acquisitions were also beneficial to certain movements like the Eclecticism of the Second Empire or the Academic Art of the Third Republic, whose significance was reassessed, allowing for, among other things, the return of the works of art until then dispersed.

Some areas, neglected by others, were the objects of particular attention. The decorative arts, practically non-existent, required significant purchases, sometimes backed by donors (the Gallé collection, for example, in 1986-1987). This showed in the quality of the Art Nouveau collections, as much in its French expression as in its different international movements: Jugenstil, Sécession, etc.

Photography was also greatly enriched. 160 portraits by Félix Nadar were purchased, and the museum also received some 1,200 daguerreotypes and photographs as a gift from the Kodak-Pathé Foundation. Architecture was not to be forgotten either. In addition to some purchases in the art market, an extraordinary Eiffel collection was given to the Museum in 1989 for the centenary of the eponymous tower.

The history of the Orsay Museum collections cannot be told in these few pages. Speaking of their quality can sometimes hide their weaknesses. This also highlights the fact that the success of Orsay, while benefiting the art market, rendered its major pieces priceless. Surely, the wealth of Orsay is so great that it can claim to bear witness to the complexity and diversity of artistic creation between 1848 and 1914.

VINCENT
VAN GOGH

Doctor Gachet

1890 / Oil on canvas

"Because realism is!"

FROM THE 1848 REVOLUTION TO 1870

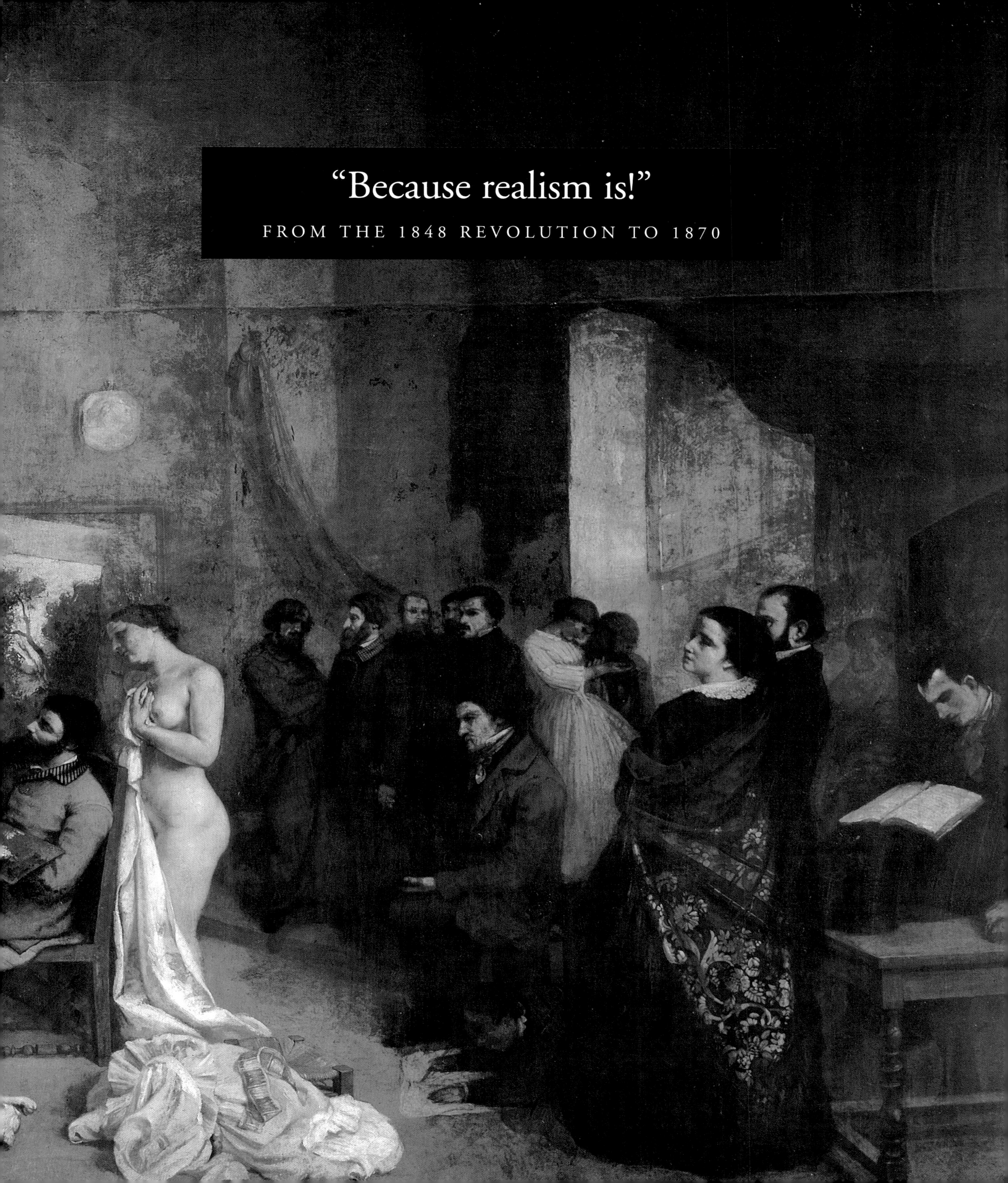

Preceding pages
GUSTAVE
COURBET

Thz Artist's Studio
*A True Allegory
Concerning Seven Years
of my Artistic Life*

1855 / Oil on canvas
141 × 235 in.

In a letter to his friend, Champfleury, Courbet explained his work: "It is the moral and physical story of my studio, part one; these are the people who help me, who support me in my idea, who participate in my work. These are the people who feed on life, who feed on death. It is society at its highest, its lowest, and in the middle. In short, it is my way of seeing society, its interests and passions. It is the world that comes to be painted at my place [...] the scene is at my studio in Paris. The painting is divided into two parts. I am in the middle, painting. To the right, those who support the actions of the painter, that is to say the friends, workers, and amateurs in the world of art. To the left, the other world of trivial life, the people, the misery, the poverty, the wealth, the exploited, the exploiters, the people who feed on death."

The Republic of France was proclaimed on February 25, 1848, following three days of insurrection. Very soon, however, economic uncertainty and political instability set the stage for the future Napoleon's rise to power. Elected president that same year, thanks to the *Parti de l'Ordre* that included both conservatives and moderates, he orchestrated the coup d'état of December 2, 1851, acceding to the Imperial throne one year later.

Twenty years later, on September 2, 1870, the French army surrendered to the Prussians and the Second Empire collapsed at Sedan. The Third Republic was proclaimed on the 4th of September.

This is the historical context, the background. Between these two events, from 1848 to 1870, France experienced a period of unquestionable economic and industrial expansion, which contrasted with the cultural conservatism of the bourgeois elite. During these years, artistic activity was the fruit of continuity and modernity.

The apparent severity of David's Neo-Classicism engendered the cults of line and form as well as the effervescence of color coming from Ingres and Delacroix. The Classicism of the former and the Romanticism of the latter lived on in this quarter of a century, and their reputations were established at the 1855 International Exhibition; this was certainly recognition, but this recognition was already frittering away.

The Events of the Exhibition

Ingres' triumph was attaining perfection, a certain idea of beauty that was pursued by students like Amaury-Duval and Hippolyte Flandrin, and that gave rise to Academic Art, which was idolized by republican notables. But of all the achievements of this period, Delacroix's was the greatest, and young artists were fervent: "The result is there, visible, immense, flamboyant," Baudelaire exclaimed.

At the Exhibition, other schools that were to coexist until the end of the century, or even beyond, made their marks. These included landscape painting—that year, the Emperor purchased a work by Corot—which played a major role in the evolution of art. But also the Orientalism of Decamps, the Patriotism of Meissonier, not to mention the tulles, silks, velours, and guipures of Winterhalter's society painting, where Empress Eugenie's maidens of honor danced under an asparagus-colored sky. While the 1855 International Exhibition assembled the movements of the Second Empire, another artistic event took place only a few feet away. Written on the front door of a pavilion erected by Courbet, to

protest against his ostracism by the jury, was the following: "Realism. Courbet. Exhibition of forty paintings from his works." There one rediscovered *Burial at Ornans*, painted a year after the Revolution of 1848, a manifesto of Realism that marked the painter's "debut" and his "statement of principles" as he put it. *Les Baigneuses* and *The Artist's Studio* were also displayed.

"You want me to paint angels..."

What was this Realism? Champfleury made this remark to George Sand: "I will not define Realism for you, Madame; I do not know where it comes from, where it is going, what it is; Homer would be a realist because he observed and described with exactitude the everyday life of his time." So, it was about a break from Academic Art that reveled in mythological and warrior subjects. It was necessary to go back to painters of the 17th Century, such as Le Nain and Hollandais, who were the initiators of this style. It was important to return to reality. Courbet's whole attitude was summed up in his famous witticism: "You want me to paint angels: show me one!"

So to be Realist "because Realism is", as Courbet said, laying claim on a term imposed on him, was not to opt for a "realist" representation of the subject, but to convey the real world. Baudelaire stated that a real painter must "see and understand... how great and poetic we are in our ties and patent boots."

Realism was not a style, it was more an attitude. In 1849, a meeting was held at the Brasserie Andler of all the artists who supported Realism, a wide assortment of personalities, such as painters like Corot, Courbet and Daumier, and sculptors like Barye and Préault.

The Birth of Modern Painting

The big event of the years 1840-1870 was the conquest of the real. Under the extensive banner of one word, Courbet, who called himself "Courbetist, that's all!" was just as realist as the painters of the Barbizon school or Manet.

It was precisely Manet, just as arrogant as his distinguished elder during the first *Salon des refusés* in 1863 (literally, the Salon of the Refused, those being the artists who were not accepted in the "official" salon), who exhibited *Le Déjeuner sur l'herbe*. He was the talk of the town. He confided to a friend, "Well it looks like I should do a nude. OK. I'll do one for them. In the transparency of the atmosphere, with people like the ones we see down there." But critics thought otherwise: "In the middle of a shady wood, a young lady stripped of all clothing chats with students in berets. Mr. Manet is a student of Goya and Baudelaire. He has already gained the repulsion of the bourgeoisie: this is a big step." wrote Monselet in *Le Figaro*. In fact, through all the noise and scandal, it was actually the birth of modern painting that was being witnessed.

Manet was a realist, a painter of modern life. But Zola preferred to refer to him as a "Naturalist". His essential contribution consisted in turning the descriptive space of the painting into an emotional space, emanating from a sensation born of the vivacity of touch, the intensity of colors, and the "transparency of the atmosphere". Manet's revolution was similar to this verse by Boileau: "If my weighty flesh were of thought." It was of the flesh of painting, of its materialism, that emotion was suddenly born, and no longer, or no longer only, of representation alone.

Manet completed the split. In view of his impetuousness, Baudelaire, observant and open to this modernity that he too advocated, was dumbfounded. He admitted, "You are but the first on the path to the degeneration of your art." Like Baudelaire, it was art that was disoriented, art that now started out on a fresh course towards Impressionism beginning at the end of the 1860s, and towards "pure painting" in the following century when all reference to reality disappeared.

Persistences, Splits and New Beginnings

Art was not a predetermined path, which led, in the 19th century, from David to Cézanne. It would be peremptory to claim that Picasso inaugurated a 20th century that also ended with him. All of art history is made up of persistences, splits and new beginnings, but in each era, they have a different impact.

When the visitor to the Orsay Museum contemplates *The Romans of the Decadence*, this vast "machine" painted by Thomas Couture, he or she may wonder what remains of the Baron Gros' studio, where the painter came from, and what kind of impression he made on Manet, his student. But it makes you wonder, when you hear Renoir say that Couture was "almost a revolutionary. Those who prided themselves on 'forging ahead' claimed to follow Couture who, in 1847, arrived on the scene like a thunderbolt with *The Romans of the Decadence*."

Thus, the Second Empire is full of questions that history seems to sort out, but that a museum must bring back to light. It is also full of diehards who seem to be born artists. None of them ever joined any of the movements they came into contact with: Corot, Daumier, Fantin-Latour, and later Edgar Degas, all great artists, without any real lineage but whose widespread influence was no less significant.

But the Orsay collections, and even more so the history of art during the Second Empire, cannot be restricted to painting alone. It is certainly a basic reflection of the evolution of sensibility, but its influence can also be found in other disciplines, which experienced the same phenomena of persistences, splits and new beginnings. First, sculpture, represented by the works exhibited in the great central nave of the museum; private works and ceremonial works, covering the 25-year period in question. From Préault's Romanticism to Pradier's Classicism, from Cavelier's antiquities to Falguière the neo-Florentine or the eclectic Cordier, the sculpture of this imperial era leads us to young Rodin's *The Man with a Broken Nose*, rejected by the 1864 Salon. Apollinaire reminds us who really dominated this period.

"Three sculptors, three stone carvers [who] give geogonic blocks the appearance of life: François Rude, Barye and Carpeaux. [...] Carpeaux, whose strong, simple grace rises up in agile groups whose delicate mass contains more refined spirit than any other relief work. I will also have to once again praise Barye, who is without doubt the greatest sculptor of the 19th century."

Even though "isms" began to flourish, showing the diversity of styles, there was one creative field that demonstrated a certain coherence: decorative arts and furniture, where blended styles dominated, and led to just one, Eclecticism. Eclecticism was also seen in architecture, with Garnier who won the 1861 competition to build the Paris Opéra. Only a few, like Viollet-le-Duc, dared counter this decorative confusion with rationalist ideas and a quest for unity of style. But this ornamental exhilaration might seem paradoxical, if one did not think of the function of these objects and their purchasers, certainly more reluctant towards these "rebels" of art than they were towards Cabanel, for example, where Botticelli, Raphaël, Ingres and Boucher rubbed shoulders.

The era was therefore tempted to flee from reality in the abundance of stuccoes and the exuberance of decorations of nimble nymphs swathed in the halos of our "dear masters". But reality was always there, lurking, in life and in literature, which Balzac and Zola praised generously. It was present, more than ever, since individuals would soon have to bear its weight on themselves: in 1837, Louis Daguerre produced the first photographic portrait of a man.

33

Facing page

View of the gallery where the retrospective of the works of Ingres was organized during the 1855 International Exhibition in Paris.

THOMAS COUTURE

The Romans of the Decadence

1847 / Oil on canvas 186 × 304 in.

Just like Géricault's *Raft of the Medusa* had been associated with the collapse of France in 1830, this work was given a political meaning by its contemporaries. One year later, in 1848, the Revolution occurred.

Painting

The major movements in painting from the years 1848-1870 are present at the Orsay Museum. It would be impossible to mention them all in such a limited space, because they cannot be strictly classified. Moreover, most of them extend beyond the Empire, or reached their apogee during the Third Republic. Already at their peak, Classicism and Romanticism opened the period. The former is the triumph of lines and the firmness of composition, the latter of movement and the supremacy of color.

CLASSICISM, dominated by Ingres, influenced painters like Amaury-Duval, Bougereau, Cabanel and Meissonier, specialists in mythology, history, and society portraits. Their respect for the dogmata of the Academy of Fine Arts earned them, under the Republic, the name *académistes* or, more affectionately, the nickname "our dear masters". The Neo-Greeks (the "Meticulous") of Gérôme or the Eclecticism of Couture can also be related to Classicism.

ROMANTICISM, stemming mostly from Delacroix, earned its reputation in this period, and developed disciples like Paul Huet and Chassériau. Later, as the movement began to fade, Delacroix's influence spread beyond his own circle: painters from the Impressionists to Fauvists were all influenced by his work.

ORIENTALISM, the expression of an Orient often cloaked in myth, inspired by Ingres' odalisques and Delacroix's voyage to Morocco, brings together all of the movements: while it is Romantic with Fromentin, Guillaumet and Tournemine added more exotic tendencies.

LANDSCAPE PAINTING, also known as *pleinairisme* (outdoorism*)*, designates a group of artists who, beginning in the 1840s, painted scenes from real life: Corot and his friends from the Barbizon school—Rousseau, Daubigny and Millet—settled at the edge of Fontainebleau Forest. The conjunction between landscape painting and Realism would soon pave the way for Impressionism.

REALISM, first appearing in the 1840s in reaction to academic art, is an ambiguous term for such different styles as Daumier, Courbet and Manet—the latter was often referred to as a Naturalist because he was much more sensitive to the study of esthetics than to any social theme. Other realist movements, at times "rustic" or "truist" could be included here, like Pils, Ribot or the early Van Gogh. But in this focus on reality, certain artists remain unclassifiable, like Fantin-Latour, at times Symbolist, or Degas.

SYMBOLISM was, like the Realism of which it was to be the antidote, less a school than an attitude. "Only that which one has never seen and shall never see should be painted." wrote Tristan Corbière. The precursors of Symbolism were Gustave Moreau and Puvis de Chavannes, but their expression would only be recognized at the end of the century.

IMPRESSIONISM came to life at the end of the 1860s, a result of the rupture initiated by Manet, and the discovery of fleeting variations of light by Jongkind and Boudin. In the beginning, there were painters like Monet, Bazille, Renoir, all in their twenties. They all worked at Fontainebleau and all were friends of Courbet and Manet.

JEAN-AUGUSTE-DOMINIQUE INGRES

The Source

1856 / Oil on canvas, 64 × 31 in.

At seventy-five, Ingres painted *The Source*, which depicts a young girl whose body flows with the same fluidity as the water. The legacy of neo-classical rigor, the purity of line and design, does not change the sensual delight that springs from the sinuous curves of the model. Of this ode to sensuality, Théophile Gautier wrote, "Innocence, youth, freshness, beauty! Unspoiled life, immaculate perfection! Palpitation and blushing in Paros marble!"

"The Lion Hunt is a veritable explosion of colors...
no colors could ever be more beautiful, more intense,
penetrating your soul through the channel of your eyes."
Charles Baudelaire
1855 International Exhibition.

EUGÈNE DELACROIX

The Lion Hunt

1854 / Study, oil on canvas, 34 × 45 in.

To Ingres' quest for the perfection of form, Delacroix responded with the exuberance of colored materials and
tumultuous movement. *The Lion Hunt* (partially damaged in 1870), conserved at the Bordeaux Museum of Fine Arts,
was preceded by this dazzling study exhibited at the Orsay Museum. Delacroix's Romanticism was pushed here
to the limits of exhilaration, and went beyond the simple name of the school: it marked the liberation of light
and color, of which the Impressionists were the principal protagonists.

*"[The painting] was painted by two men
with completely different personalities...
The young Greeks are in marble, the roosters are flesh
and bone; the characters are painted in the Gleyre method,
the animals from nature."*
Champfleury.

JEAN-LÉON GÉRÔME

The Cockfight

1846 / Oil on canvas, 56 × 80 in.

Student of Delaroche and Gleyre—at the studio where Renoir and Monet studied—Gérôme was one of the most famous artists
of his times. He owed his first success to his *Cockfight*, of which Gautier praised the "rare elegance" and "exquisite distinction". The poet
invented the term "Neo-Greeks" and "Pompeians", referring to Gérôme and his friends, partisans of a meticulously realistic and smooth
method of painting. Painter as well as sculptor (see his *Tanagra* at the Orsay Museum), fanatic of Academic Art, of which he was more
the patron than a simple advocate, Gérôme was also one of the most outspoken critics of Impressionism.

THÉODORE CHASSÉRIAU

The Tepidarium

1853 / Oil on canvas, 67 × 102 in.

Chasseriau depicted the Venus Genitrix baths at Pompeii, or more precisely the tepidarium, a bath kept at moderate
temperatures, between that of the calidarium (hot bath) and the frigidarium (cold bath). Souvenirs of his trip to the Orient
mix with Roman themes. Pupil of Ingres, whose design he adopted, Chasseriau's art later evolved towards movement and
sustained colorings, influenced by Delacroix, and exacerbated by his excitement for the discovery of Algeria in 1846.
This blending of cultures reunites here the styles of his two masters: the sharpness of line and the vibration of color.

38

HONORÉ DAUMIER

Crispin and Scapin

circa 1858-1860 / Oil on canvas, 24 × 32 in.

"This guy's a little Michelangelo," affirmed Balzac in 1830. As a caricaturist, he took incisive lines and devastating caricatures to the levels of great art. He was known as a sculptor as well, amusing himself with figures of parliament members. As a painter, Daumier was not well known among his colleagues. He was a Realist by disposition and Republican by conviction, but his style cannot be classified, made up of a curious mix of forms and lines, sober, vague and uncontrollable. In *Crispin and Scapin*, two theater characters, Daumier used framing, light and contrasts that Degas later reproduced in his own work.

JEAN-FRANÇOIS MILLET

The Angelus

1857-1859 / Oil on canvas, 22 × 26 in.

Few works could have been so burnt out by celebrity. Yet, what a work! In *The Angelus*, life is cloistered,
reassured by its culmination, by the order of things. Under a "cottony and melancholic sky", wrote Gambetta,
only the woman prays, glorified by the light; the shadowy mass of the man waits in meditation. They are two nuances
of devotion that amplify the spiritual dimension of the meek. Millet expressed an end-of-century nostalgia,
an agony that the artist himself witnessed, as the furious machinery of the new industrial world was rumbling.

"Corot's 'imaginative' freshness when he paints,
released from the anxiety of the usual reception,
when he doesn't sacrifice to the conformist salons,
when he discovers the joys of light and shadow..."
André Masson
Le Plaisir de peindre, 1950.

CAMILLE COROT

The Dance of the Nymphs

circa 1850-1851 / Oil on canvas, 39 × 52 in.

Born in 1796, Corot was deeply influenced by the first landscape painters like Michallon, Bertin, and d'Aligny who,
well before the Impressionists, set up their easels in the outdoors, aware that it was light that animated life.
No school could attach its name to Corot; all movements seemed to converge in him.
This tireless voyager was Classical for his precocious touch, Romantic for his lyricism, Realist for his precision and sincerity.
But these diversities seem to be assembled, united by a light veil of melancholic, meditative delusions.

FRANZ XAVER
WINTERHALTER

**Madame
Rimsky-Korsakov**

1864 / Oil on canvas
46 × 35 in.

Of German descent,
Winterhalter rapidly
became one
of the official painters
of the French Court,
and one of the idolized
society portraitists of the
Second Empire—a genre
that was just as popular
under the Republic.
Sometimes theatrical,
other times languorous,
portraits were available
in all styles, illustrated
by its promoters, Cabanel,
Bonnat, Carolus-Duran
or Amaury-Duval.
Although a prisoner
of the genre, Winterhalter's
art always demonstrated
great virtuosity
in conveying
the refinement of fabrics,
and of clothes, while
endowing his models
with expressions of intense
sensuality and vivacity. ·

ALEXANDRE CABANEL

The Birth of Venus

circa 1863 / Oil on canvas, 51 × 89 in.

The year when Manet exhibited *Le Déjeuner sur l'herbe,* considered obscene, Cabanel's *Birth of Venus*
was praised at the official Salon. The Emperor immediately acquired it. Four years later,
during a new presentation of the painting, Zola wrote, "See *The Birth of Venus* at Champ-de-Mars.
The goddess, submerged in a river of milk, looks like a delicious libertine, not in flesh
and bone—that would be indecent—, but in a sort of white and pink almond paste."

*"Like a man who falls in the snow, Manet
has made an impression on public opinion."*
Champfleury to Baudelaire.

ÉDOUARD MANET

Le Déjeuner sur l'herbe

1863 / Oil on canvas, 82 × 104 in.

Object of scandal in 1863, at the *Salon des refusés*, the work (then entitled *The Bath*) marked a transitional period in the history
of painting: it paved the way for Impressionism, it was the departure point for modern art. Zola described it in 1867: "It's not the picnic
on the grass that you must see in the painting, it's the entire landscape, with its vigor and its subtlety, with its large, solid foregrounds
and its lightly delicate backdrops; it is this firm flesh, shaped by big patches of light, its supple and strong fabrics, and most of all this
delicious silhouette of a woman in shirtsleeves who, in the back, creates an adorable white spot in the middle of green leaves."

HENRI FANTIN-LATOUR

A Studio in Batignolles

1870 / Oil on canvas, 80 × 108 in.

In 1863, Fantin-Latour painted his *Hommage à Delacroix* (at the Orsay Museum), testimony to the recognition that the new generation held for the master. Seven years later, with his *Studio in Batignolles*, he paid homage to Manet. Surrounding Manet, at his easel, one recognizes Renoir—who is only 22 years old at the time—whose face is detached from the frame; Zola, at his side, speaks to Bazille, behind whom, on the far right of the painting, stands Monet—only 23 years old himself. Except for his eccentric personality, Fantin-Latour admired Manet, just like he loved these young Impressionists who were beginning to make themselves known. But his work is above all introspective, intimist. He excelled at creating relationships between forms and colors. In the silence of the painting there is both independence and complicity in the faces, animated by the same intellectual and moral fervor.

Sculpture

The sculpture of the Second Empire, in an abundance of styles, experienced the introduction of new techniques and new materials. The predominance of marble was questioned, and smoothness, which seemed to be consubstantial with sculpture, slowly gave way to sensual manipulation of material by hand, allowing the material to express itself, its nature and spontaneity. As in painting, the 1840s begin with two dominant movements: Classicism and Romanticism.

CLASSICISM is found in the work of James Pradier, where the sobriety of monumental works contrasts with the less conventional attitude of *Sapho* or the intimist grace of his smaller statues. Although Pradier, who died in 1852, belonged more to the previous generation, Classicism still underwent a renewed vitality, with artists like Guillaume or Cavelier.

ROMANTICISM was also as present as ever, with David d'Angers, Préault and Rude, he who so well defined its spirit with a few words on one of his works, "There is something in there that chills my own soul." One of the century's geniuses is linked to this movement: Barye, the artist so well known for his sculptures of animals.

ECLECTICISM, that is, the absorption of different styles in the composition of a work, can be found in the neo-Florentines, a movement parallel to the return to Classicism. Its best known artists are Falguière, Mercié and Dubois, with refined formalism marked by the return to classical antiquity, and an admiration for the Italian Renaissance. Eclecticism can also be found in the works of Clésinger, whose *Woman Bitten by a Snake* incited Delacroix to say "It is a Daguerreotype in sculpture." Eclecticism also included works often associated with Orientalism, where polychromy and combined materials appear, as in the works of Charles Cordier, who mixed bronze, onyx and porphyry in his *Nègre de Soudan*—a formula that prospered under the Third Republic.

REALISM was equally present. It appeared already in the 1830s, but really established itself after the Commune. Daumier's statuary can be linked to Realism, his parliamentary busts in clay or the bronze *Ratapoil*, which, in 1850, satirized the *parti de l'Ordre*. With his treatment of volumes, sense of movement, presence of lines in the modeling—he was a real precursor of Rodin.

BEYOND all of these movements, the dominant figure was Carpeaux. His elegance blossomed in large public decors and in his portraits. Apollinaire was not mistaken when he wrote, "Later it will be recognized that the Second Empire was an era of style. The purest expression of this artistic style is found in the works of the sculptor Carpeaux, who was, more than anyone else, the man of his time."

FRANÇOIS RUDE

The Spirit of the Motherland

1836 / Plaster
88 × 77 × 35 in.

45

This bust, commissioned in 1887 by the city of Dijon—birthplace of Rude—is a high relief casting from the *Arc de Triomphe* in Paris, entitled *Departure of the Volunteers of 1792*, also known as *La Marseillaise*. François Rude, Romantic in his inspiration, Realist in his sense of observation, died in 1855. Apollinaire, who described him as one of the greatest sculptors of the century, said of his *Marseillaise,* "[it] is the first work that expresses some modern sublimity, the subject is modern, the movement, life is modern in it and the synthetic dramatization of that which is represented in it is also modern."

ANTOINE-LOUIS
BARYE

**Tartan Warrior
on Horse**

1855 / Bronze
2 × 5,5 × 14 in.

An acute observer, Barye
associated precision
of execution with a sense
of movement displayed in
his animal work. Delacroix,
who loved Barye, was
happy to model with him.
"Mr. Barye does not treat
animals through a purely
zoological point of view;
when he does a lion,
a tiger, a bear or an
elephant, he is not content
with being exact and true
to the highest degree;
he knows that the
reproduction of nature does
not necessarily make art;
he enlarges, he simplifies,
he idealizes animals and
gives them some style;
he has a very proud,
energetic, severe way about
him that makes him
like the Michelangelo
of animals."
Théophile Gautier.

JEAN-BAPTISTE
known as
AUGUSTE
CLÉSINGER

**Woman Bitten
by a Snake**

1847 / Marble
22 × 71 × 22 in.

The work was produced
from a casting taken
of Apollonie Sabatier, also
known as *La Présidente*,
Baudelaire's "muse and
Madonna"—it is she who
is shown at the far right
of Courbet's *Studio*,
in front of Baudelaire who
is seated (see pp. 30-31).
Though Clésinger was
quite successful, he often
encountered criticism.
The sensual delight
of the woman was not to
everyone's liking.
The sculptor toned down
the effect of these amorous
convulsions by adding
a snake to the work
and giving it
an insignificant title.

JEAN-BAPTISTE
CARPEAUX
The Dance

1866-1869 / Échaillon
stone
165 × 117 × 57 in.

A student of Rude,
Carpeaux first made
himself known for
his *Ugolin and her Children*
(at the Orsay Museum).
Close to the imperial
family, this envious
situation allowed him
to obtain a great number
of public commissions.
The group in *The Dance*,
meant to decorate the
façade of the Paris Opéra,
was unveiled in 1869
to the sound of booing by
the right-thinking society.
People spoke of these six
"epileptic" figures, which
smelt of "vice, stinking
of wine". The work was
splattered with black ink.
Its removal was demanded.
The very thing that made
it beautiful is criticized: the
realism—when the general
public was used to cold
allegories—the movement,
the liveliness, the quivering
joy, the ability to extract
from stone a feeling
of grace and agility
conferred on these five
women who surround
a masculine genie.
Damaged by atmospheric
pollution, the work
was moved to the Louvre
in 1964, then to Orsay,
replaced by a copy
by Paul Belmondo.

Photography

WITH SEVERAL thousand works, the Orsay Museum collections cover the field of photography from the "primitive era"—the years 1840-1870, according to Nadar—up to the beginning of the 20th century, when it acquired it artistic autonomy.

THE FIRST EVIDENCE of photography—called heliography—dates back to 1826-1827: a view of rooftops taken by Nicéphore Niépce from the window of his home. This crowned the work he had begun in 1816. But it was not until the invention of Louis Daguerre's process that a decisive impetus was given, and his daguerreotype was presented to the public—in 1989, one of his daguerreotypes from 1837 was found: the first photographic portrait.

THE 1840s had only just marked the triumph of this process—which allowed for only one print on a copper plate—when an attempt was already made to substitute it with the negative-positive technique on paper. The work of people like the Englishman Henry Fox Talbot and the Frenchman Hippolyte Bayard permitted the progressive replacement, during the 1850s, of the restricting daguerreotype, thanks to the pioneering work of Bayard himself, Le Gray, Nègre, Le Secq, and Marville.

SO, DURING THE SECOND EMPIRE, with the help of constant technical evolutions (albumin and collodion, glass plates, etc.) photography came out of its limbo and undertook the road to industrialization. Color was the order of the day: in 1862, Ducos du Hauron laid down the principles of chromaphotography, which did not have much practical application until the beginning of the 20th century, with the Lumière brothers' autochromes.

IN ITS EARLY STAGES, photography benefited from several initiatives to promote it. Strong support was given to it by public authorities, beginning in 1839, then in 1851 with the creation of the Heliographic Society, and later, in 1859, the admittance of photography at the Salon, shown next to painting and sculpture. These places of discussion, frequented by practitioners and scientists, writers and artists like Gautier and Delacroix, encouraged practical confrontation and theoretical reflection by examining the function of photography: scientific (archiving architectural patrimony), documentary (describing society), factual (documenting natural catastrophes or conflicts), and artistic (reproducing landscapes, designing still-lifes, making portraits).

IN THE MIDST of this feverish innovation, beyond just the technical aspects, the new art raised some concerns of a philosophical nature, dealing with reality and its mirror, realism and imagination, the role of the painter and that of the photographer. In 1850, Delacroix likened the latter to "a machine harnessed to another machine". Seven years later, Nadar retorted with these words, "Photography is a marvelous discovery, a science that occupies the greatest intellects, an art that arouses the shrewdest of minds—and whose application is within reach of the dumbest of imbeciles [...]. Photographic theory can be learned in an hour [...]. I will tell you cannot be learned: the feeling for light, the artistic appreciation of the effects produced by different and combined days, the application of this or that effect according to the nature of the features that you the artist must reproduce. What can be learned even less is the moral intelligence of your subject, the rapid touch with which you commune with the model."

FÉLIX TOURNACHON called NADAR

Portrait of Baudelaire

circa 1855 / Salted paper from a glass collodion negative, 9.5 × 7 in.

In his desire to not confuse "art and industry", Baudelaire always held a critical attitude towards photography. Nevertheless, several portraits remain of the poet: some by Étienne Carjat, but mostly by Nadar. Here the negative was miraculously "messed up"; it shows a slight tremble—due to a rather difficult pose of nearly twenty seconds—from which emerges a strange presence, the feeling that reality emerges from this frozen mobility. Caricaturist, journalist, hot air balloonist (model for Jules Verne's Captain Ardan), Nadar opened his photography studio in 1854. It was there that the first Impressionist exhibition took place in 1874.

"I love clouds... clouds floating by...
over there... over there... marvelous clouds"
Charles Baudelaire, *The Stranger*, 1862.

GUSTAVE LE GRAY

Steam

1857 / Albumin paper from a glass collodion negative.

A student of the painter Delaroche, Le Gray was one of the artisans who abandoned the daguerreotype
in favor of paper and glass negatives. He played a key role in French photography in the 1850s, training men like
Henri Le Secq and Adrien Tournachon, Nadar's brother. Because of its quality, and its themes (the sea, the forests),
Le Gray's work rapidly opened the debate about the legitimacy of photography as artistic creation.

Decorative Arts

CAN THE SECOND EMPIRE be credited with the creation of a certain style? The period following the *Monarchie de Juillet* actually displays certain continuity. If any rupture took place, it is to be attributed to the society under the reign of Louis-Philippe. The taste for antiquities so dear to the First Empire, and the clarity and sobriety of lines that exemplified the Restoration, was abandoned by the bourgeois monarchy of Louis-Philippe. He alternately became infatuated with Gothic, Renaissance, Louis XIII and rocaille styles, following literary fashions, through the historical novels of Walter Scott, Victor Hugo and Alexandre Dumas, historical works or archeological excavations.

UNDER THE SECOND EMPIRE fashion also gave way to "historicity": neo-Renaissance, neo-Louis XIV, then neo-Regency and, neo-Louis XVI, the favored "neo". There was a recycling of earlier formulas, including furniture in papier mâché or the mythical tuft that overwhelmed living rooms, while turning towards different styles. They accumulated abundantly in architecture and interior decoration, they mixed and got muddled up in objects, only to form one style: Eclecticism, from the name of a contemporary philosophical doctrine advocating the conciliation and absorption of different theories into one system.

OPULENCE IN DECORATION was followed by opulence in consumption. From Zola's *Ladies' Pleasure*, to Printemps and Samaritaine, the *Grands Magasins* (Parisian department stores) developed. Mass production and commerce grew. The ornamental vocabulary widened, including more vegetable and mineral elements; people could not resist the seduction of exoticism.

THESE RADICAL CHANGES obviously depended on economical and industrial progress. Production increased at lower costs, beauty extended to utility: in 1864, the future Museum of Decorative Arts opened to the public. The gigantic International Exhibitions, inaugurated for the first time at London's Crystal Palace, in 1851, drew considerable crowds. 11 million visitors attended the Exhibition held in Paris in 1867. That year, Japanese art was introduced to the public; Japanese art spread to all artistic activities becoming, at the end of the century, one of the foundations of Art nouveau.

NO AREA OF DECORATION was ignored. Furniture experienced the evolution of its lines that imposed on the most popular establishments or cabinetmakers, like Fourdinois, Gouhé and Diehl, who called on designers or sculptors to ensure the right decor. The goldsmith trade also intersected styles, combining bronze with ivory, copper with enamel and gems for the rich clientele of Froment-Meurice. At Christofle, they preferred to "play" with "reserved elegance", offering silverware at unusual prices: thanks to new developments in electroplating, a coat of gold or silver could be applied, by electrolysis, to the surface of less expensive metals. The porcelains of Sèvres, Limoges and Paris were still valued and in vogue. Glassware, be it from Baccarat or the Cristalleries de Saint-Louis, competed with audacity and ingenuity. Translucent, transparent, colored and engraved, it offered new forms in harmony with the decor, it revived styles of the past that it copied or interpreted and made fashionable again: Bohemian and Venetian glassware. Was there a Second Empire style? Without a doubt, but it is a paradoxical style, which incorporated elements of all styles into the exhilrated decor.

CHARLES LEPEC, *painter*
CH. DOTIN, *enameller*

Decorative panel: "Clémence Isaure"
.
1865 / Copper painted with enamel, gold-plated copper, 71 × 44 in.

A legendary character, to whom the creation, in the 14th century, of the *Jeux floraux* of Toulouse is attributed, the presence of Clémence Isaure in this decoration was characteristic of a return to the Middle Ages, an era which, like the Orient, stimulated the imagination of many an artist. The Second Empire was also fond of rediscovering abandoned materials and techniques, among which were enamel paints in the Renaissance style.

THÉODORE DECK

Monumental Cup

circa 1870
Faience
23 × 16 in.

Eclecticism can be historical and spatial. Since the beginning of the century, France had discovered orientalism, especially in painting. With Deck, the Orient influenced the decorative arts. Keen connoisseur of Iznik's earthenware and Chinese ceramics, he often incorporated this type of repertoire into themes and forms borrowed from the Renaissance.

CHARLES DIEHL, *cabinet maker* / JEAN BRANDELY, *designer*
EMMANUEL FREMIET, *sculptor*

Médaillier

1867 / Cedar, marquetry in walnut, ebony and ivory on an oak frame, silver-plated bronze and copper, 94 × 59 × 24 in.

Fremiet—Rude's nephew—, who was known for his animal statuary and his taste for archeological reconstructions, decorated this médaillier, presented at the 1867 International Exhibition. The theme here is *The Triumphant Entry of Mérovée to Châlons-sur-Marne*. Fremier had already made a name for himself at the 1864 Salon with his "authentic" *Gaulish Chief* on horseback. During the 1860s, the excavations of Alesia began.

"The magnificent poetry
of the passing moment"

THE IMPRESSIONIST YEARS

Preceding pages

CLAUDE
MONET

Saint-Lazare Station

1877 / Oil on canvas
(detail)
30 × 41 in.

Having set up his easel in
the Saint-Lazare Station,
Monet painted a dozen
canvases. A witness
reported, "He relentlessly
painted the departure
of the locomotives [...].
Not comfortable with the
maneuvers, he stayed there,
his brush on the lookout,
like a hunter, watching
out for the moment
of his brushstroke."
At the exhibition of seven
of his paintings during
the Impressionist
exhibition of 1877,
Émile Zola wrote,
"You can hear the
rumbling of the trains
entering the station,
you can see the outpouring
of vapors that roll under
the vast hangars [...].
Our artists need to find
the poetry of train stations
like their fathers found
that of forests and rivers."

On April 15, 1874 the first Impressionist exhibition opened to the public at Nadar's studio, located in Paris, at 35, boulevard des Capucines. Two weeks before the official Salon, a requisite passage for all artists, the event had all the makings of a protest. Thirty exhibitors and 165 paintings were displayed. Monet, Renoir, Sisley, Degas, Morisot, Pissarro, Cézanne, Guillaumin, Boudin, and Jongkind were present. While the latter two were already in their fifties, the others were between thirty and forty years old. Manet, a longtime supporter of his friends, did not, however, wish to participate, considering that the battle was to be fought at the Salon where "my worst enemies are forced to file past my canvases."

In the April 25th edition of *Le Charivari*, Louis Leroy, who spoke of "palette scrapings", coined the term Impressionist, through analogy—more through derision—of Monet's painting *Impression, Sunrise.* He wrote, "Impression, I was sure of it. I also thought that because I am impressed, there must be some impression in there." No matter, the word was accepted. But how did we arrive at this point?

The Sources of Impressionism

Impressionism is not really a school. The term refers to a behavior in relation to nature, an aptitude for observation and the retention of the many fleeting variations of light; the ability to transmit the feeling of a suspension of time. Élie Faure was right when he wrote, "It is the visual sensation of an instant, which a long and patient analysis of the quality of light and elements of color has permitted three or four men to immortalize their infinite and ever-changing complexity." Gustave Geffroy, Monet's biographer, concurred when he spoke of "the magnificent poetry of the passing moment".

But Impressionism is not a movement conceived ex nihilo, it stems from a great number of movements, through a lineage whose coherence is at times difficult to reconstruct. The contribution of Romanticism, for example, is undeniable. Not the romantic imagery that belonged to mythology, Shakespearean theater, historical themes or exoticism, but the romanticism of emancipation, the audacity of execution and masses of color. It was Delacroix's romanticism that was able to bring out the emotion of chromatic vertigo.

Another important source is landscape painting, whose relation Renoir summed up in a few short words, "These trees, this sky... I know but three painters who could convey this: Claude Lorrain, Corot and Cézanne." Exalted as a genre in the 17th century, it had renewed popularity at the beginning of the 19th century thanks to the works of Constable, in Great Britain, and Bertin and Michallon in France. As a student of the latter, Corot acted as the mediator, perpetuator and innovator of this "atmospheric" art.

Other important landscape painters who figure in the renewal of the genre are the Barbizon painters, grouped around Théodore Rousseau in the 1840s. Two key figures must also be added: Boudin and Jongkind. Monet himself worked with Boudin at the age of seventeen, and he said of Jongkind, "I owe him for the definitive education of my eye." To the discovery of color and landscape must be added the discovery of realism, that is to say, the abandoning of the academic vision for a careful look at the themes of daily life. Idealized by Courbet, Realism evolved through the works of Manet towards a naturalism that abolished all obedience to composition in favor of pure visual sensation. It is this emotion that the Impressionists remembered, reproduced with the help of wide strokes whose energy seemed more in keeping with the rapidity and vivacity that motif work requires.

"Who is this rascal making pastiches?"

Within the context of the 1860s, a decisive period in art history, when the battle of modernity was fought, a number of young artists were imbued with these many ideas. They wandered through these movements in all directions, following acquaintances and influences, effecting the complex passage from Realism to Impressionism, from Courbet to Manet, then from Manet to Monet, the former finally being influenced by the latter.

But if we look closely, this was not an initiation ritual; the stages do not succeed each other by hierarchical layers. In these intersecting progressions, everything already seemed to settle into place in the first five years of the decade; roles evolved according to the alchemy of acquaintances and personalities.

Fantin-Latour and Whistler rubbed shoulders and associated with the English Pre-Raphaelites. Whistler was also a friend of Courbet, whom he accompanied to Trouville. Pissarro met Corot, and the young daubers—Monet, Renoir, Bazille, and Sisley—who met at Gleyre's studio towards 1860, worked in the open air at Fontainebleau, following in the footsteps of the Barbizon painters. Courbet and Monet crossed paths as early as 1859. Later, the "Realist" helped the latter with money and advice, and was a witness at his wedding in 1870. The young Renoir was himself an admirer of Courbet, and for many years paid homage to him through his work.

Édouard Manet and Baudelaire were present at Delacroix's private funeral. Degas became close friends with Manet, and visited Ingres. Everyone knew each other and went to the Salons together. For example, Courbet, Manet, Boudin, Degas, Fantin-Latour, Whistler, Monet, Pissarro, Renoir and Morisot exhibited together in 1865. That year Manet was criticized and he put the blame on the young Monet: "Who is this rascal who makes such shameful pastiches of my painting?"

Meetings, friendships and conflicts were all stimulants that fed the young generation's creative fervor. Monet echoed this, when, in 1864, settled at Honfleur, he wrote, "Every day I discover more beautiful things. I could go crazy. I have so many things I want to do, my head's bursting."

But, for a while, the guiding light was Manet. He was the one who triumphed and scandalized; the one who painted *Concert in the Tuileries Gardens* in 1860, where all the seeds of his art can be found; the one who exhibited *Le Déjeuner sur l'herbe* in 1863 at the *Salon des refusés*, and *Olympia* two years later. The future Impressionists quickly made him their leader and—as Monet reported—often had discussions with him. "He invited me to come see him every night at a café in Batignolles where he and his friends got together after work to chat. There I met Fantin-Latour and Cézanne, and Degas who arrived a bit later from Italy [...]. I brought Sisley, Bazille, and Renoir." Many other names should be added to the roster of these gatherings at Café Guerbois where, between 1866 and 1870, an incredible array of personalities mingled: Pissarro and Courbet, as well as Zola, Duranty and Nadar.

For these novice painters, the company of the more experienced artists undoubtedly led them to expand their horizons even further, to invent a language in which they had to make the rules without knowing the outcome. Among the pioneering masterpieces: *La Grenouillère*, in 1869, fruit of some of the discussions and theories at Café Guerbois. Boats and the light glistening on the water were some of the haunting themes that Monet and Renoir explored simultaneously at Bougival. Short and fragmented, the brushwork alternates values in order to restore the luminous vibrations that seem to caress the swaying surface, the foliage blends into it and the figures are but vaguely contoured silhouettes. Historian Kenneth Clark wrote, "Impressionism was born at La Grenouillère, the café on the banks of the Seine."

From Argenteuil to Giverny

War broke out in 1870. Bazille died in combat, leaving a promising career uncompleted. Renoir was mobilized. Cézanne sought refuge at l'Estaque. Manet and Degas stayed in Paris, and Monet and Pissarro went to London where they were struck by the works of Turner and Constable.

When peace returned, Monet was in France at the end of 1871. He settled in Argenteuil. Exercising a certain influence over the group, many of his friends joined him. Renoir, for whom landscape painting had already lost its interest, applied himself from then on to volumes and human representations. He used an Impressionist technique, using brushwork with a shimmering density. Sisley, the Englishman, faithful to the landscapes of the Île-de-France, showed a sensitive, almost melancholic vision, which contrasted with the firmness and colored richness of Pissarro, who settled in Pontoise, where he welcomed and supported artists like Cézanne or Guillaumin.

Manet never wished to get openly involved with the Impressionists, but they nevertheless influenced him. When he accepted to work outdoors, his palette brightened and gained luminosity. Degas, also on the fringes, more willing to grasp social reality and movement than to dedicate himself to landscapes, later became attracted to his favorite themes: the dancers of the Opéra, and racetracks. During the 1874 International Exhibition the group confirmed its cohesion, as they did at the 1876 Exhibition, supported by the merchant Durand-Ruel, and the 1877 one as well—the first one to proudly bear the title of "Impressionist Exhibition". But they only aroused jokes and jeers; critics were unanimous in mocking them.

Around 1880, this cohesion held no more. Cézanne was looking to move beyond Impressionism to better assert his own language. Since the 1879 exposition—despite the arrival of Mary Cassat and Paul Gauguin—the group was beginning to split up. Renoir's testimony was eloquent, "Around 1883, there was an abrupt change in my work. I had done everything I could with Impressionism and I had reached the conclusion that I no longer knew how to paint or draw. In short, I had reached a deadlock." Also in 1883, Monet withdrew to Giverny, working on the representation of motifs at different times, in different seasons. This was the *Rouen Cathedral* series, in 1892-1893, followed by the variations on the *Water Lilies,* in which the Father of Impressionism seems to take his art to extremes, dissolving forms into pure chromatic abstractions. Berthe Morisot organized the movement's last exhibit in 1886. Monet, Renoir, Caillebotte and Sisley refused to attend. Pissarro, faithful champion of the new generation, participated, as did Degas—on the condition that the word Impressionism be removed from the posters. The painter who dominated was without a doubt the 27 year old Georges Seurat. He presented *A Sunday Afternoon on the Island of La Grande Jatte*, a manifesto of Neo-Impressionism.

55

Facing page

Nadar's studio where the first Impressionist exhibition took place in Paris in 1874 on the top floors of 35, boulevard des Capucines. Photograph by Nadar.

PIERRE-
AUGUSTE
RENOIR

La Grenouillère

1869 / Oil on canvas,
26 × 34 in.
Stockholm,
Nationalmuseum.

Painting

IMPRESSIONISM covers two floors of the Orsay Museum.
On the ground floor, the rooms contain the Eduardo Mollard and
Antonin Personnaz collections, the Pre-Impressionists, as well as pre-
1870 works by Manet, Renoir, Bazille, Monet and Degas. In the Galerie
des Hauteurs, which begins with the Moreau-Nélaton collection, we can
see the beginnings of the movement, then its development. On these
two floors, we see that Impressionism does not have impermeable
borders. The continuation of a movement that started around 1840,
it turned up twenty years later and reached its pinnacle at the turn
of the century, when it paved the way for modern painting.

THE LANDSCAPE PAINTERS, precursors to the Impressionists,
were the Barbizon painters. But we must also include Jongkind, just
as much a painter as a watercolorist, Eugène Boudin, who wanted
"to make paintings that look like sketches," and Stanislas Lépine, whose
delicate brushstrokes translated the atmosphere and peculiar luminosity
of Paris and Normandy. Atmospheric luminosity, the "finished-
unfinished" characteristics of sketches, the lightness of watercolors,
all these were leitmotivs belonging to Impressionism.

ÉDOUARD MANET, Naturalist painter of *Olympia* and
The Balcony, portraitist of Zola and Mallarmé, or painter converted to
Impressionism—all are the same artist, the one whose "paintings
produce, as always, the impression of a wild or even an almost unripe
fruit," according to the nice metaphor of Berthe Morisot.

MONET'S WORK exemplifies the birth of Impressionism and its
completion, with the *Water Lilies* that seem to sum up what Baudelaire
said of art, "subject and object at the same time, the world outside of
the artist and the artist himself."

CAMILLE PISSARRO is the creator of a body of work that travels
through the history of the movement, from "scribbles" of hoarfrost to
his Divisionnist style of the 1880's. Often associated with Pissarro,
Sisley stands out for his subtle way of catching the harmonies between
light and color that emanate from his landscapes of the Île-de-France.
Among the myriad artists of light are Lebourg, with his pictures of Paris
and Rouen; Guillaumin, whose work, far from the serenity of Renoir,
wells up an anguish that was appreciated by Cézanne and Van Gogh;
Berthe Morisot and Mary Cassatt, whose works are moving for their
intimacy.

RENOIR EXPLORED possibilities for human representation
in Impressionism. From the young painter with the effervescent style
to the aging artist, his work is a constant hymn to life, and to the
amorous and fertile sensuality of women.

FINALLY, Cézanne who debuts with his "gutsy manner" in gloomy
colors, only to end up at the limits of a vibrant and luminous abstraction.

TO THESE NAMES, a few painters associated with Impressionism,
who refused to abolish figures just for a touch of color, should be added.
Caillebotte, for example, and Whistler, whose strange works cannot be
easily explained, with their blend of Realism, Naturalism, Symbolism
and Japanese art, that made up a refined type of Impressionism. And
Degas, many-faceted and yet unique, the artist of the movement who
admitted that "no art is so lacking in spontaneity as mine." Surprising
Degas, with his many wax statuettes (pp. 24-25), which showed that
Impressionist sculpture was possible, when Impressionism was thought
to include only the arts of drawing and painting.

CLAUDE MONET

Women in the Garden

1867 / Oil on canvas, 100 × 81 in.

Along with *Déjeuner sur l'herbe*, which he tackled in 1865, almost as a challenge to Manet's *Déjeuner sur l'herbe*,
Women in the Garden marks Monet's preoccupation with outdoor compositions that included characters.
His models? The three women on the left are one in the same: Camille, his companion.
On the right is Gabrielle, Zola's girlfriend. "These four women in white who are so different, these flowers,
this greenery, this corner of blue sky, it is youth and springtime," wrote Gustave Geffroy.

*"Not being able to embark on a grand composition, I sought to paint to the best
of my ability as simple a subject as possible. Anyway, as far as I know,
the subject is not what is important, as long as what I did is interesting from
a painting point of view. I chose the modern era because that is the one
I understand best, the one that I find the most lively for living people..."*
Frédéric Bazille.

FRÉDÉRIC BAZILLE

Family Reunion

1867 / Oil on canvas, 60 × 90 in.

On the terrace of the family home, at Méric, near Montpellier, Bazille gathered his relatives. Of this painting,
Zola wrote, "You can see that the painter loves his era, like Claude Monet, and that he thinks you can be an artist
by painting a frock coat." Even though Manet's hand is still visible here, it is no less visible in Monet's *Women
in the Garden* (preceding page), his design, his treatment of the light was a source of inspiration
for Frédéric Bazille—who was the purchaser of the painting, later in the hands of Manet.

"It was suddenly like a torn veil;
I had understood,
I had grasped what painting could be;
just by the example of this painter enamoured
of his art and of independence, my destiny
as a painter had opened up."
Claude Monet.

EUGÈNE BOUDIN

The Beach at Trouville

1867 / Oil on canvas, 12.6 × 19 in.

Noticed by Baudelaire at the 1859 Salon, the poet evoked "these studies so rapidly
and truthfully sketched from that which is the most inconstant,
the most elusive in form and in color, from waves and clouds..."
Add that to Boudin's light palette, his work on the motif and the outdoors
and Impressionism was like a seed growing in the work of this painter of Norman beaches.

JOHAN BARTHOLD JONGKIND

The Seine and Notre-Dame de Paris

1864 / Oil on canvas, 16.5 × 22 in.

Jongkind, of Dutch origin, was one of the sources of Impressionism. In 1862, he met Boudin, with whom he never
ceased to paint, and Monet. The latter was twenty-two years old, Jongkind was twenty years older,
"He was a good, simple man, abominably murdering the French language, very shy. [...] He had my my sketches
shown to him, he invited me to work with him and he explained the how and the why of his ways, rounding
out the instruction I had received from Boudin. He was from that moment my real master..."

*"The jacket of the young man, seated at right,
is similar to a summer's night sky,
all abuzz with stars."*
André Masson, *The Painter and Time,* 1946.

PIERRE-AUGUSTE RENOIR

Ball at the Moulin de la Galette, Montmartre

1876 / Oil on canvas, 51.5 × 69 in.

Painted on site, in an open-air café adjacent to the windmill in upper Montmartre, the work makes
use of the Impressionist method of reproducing physiognomy. Gustave Geffroy, art critic and friend of Renoir,
commented on the painting, "[the] exhilaration of the dance, of noise, sun, dust [...], a passionate movement, a shadow
that wins, a fire that spreads, the pleasure and the fatigue. All the poor romance heroines with the thin faces,
expressive hands, light and flighty or weary attitudes, who express hope, excitement, abandon, fierce boredom."

PIERRE-AUGUSTE RENOIR

Torso study, Effect of Sun

circa 1876 / Oil on canvas,
32 × 25.5 in.

The body is no longer
a design, but a mass
of light and color.
Its faded forms merge
with the light filtered
by abstract foliage.
In 1949, the painter
André Masson used these
terms, of magnificent
pertinence, to describe
his admiration for Renoir,
"Impressionism: often
form is only disfigured
by light. For Renoir,
the most important part
is light, but he succeeds
in creating a blended
world by inventing
a proliferation that is
sometimes disheveled
or tousled, sometimes
fluid, with attractive
centers." And he added,
"Renoir, with his very
pure force of panic,
emancipates pictorial
space. Cézanne, with
his gothic spirit,
makes people kneel
before the horizon."

*"I felt that my conscience was becoming liberated
the day that my eyes became liberated."*
Camille Pissarro.

CAMILLE PISSARRO

Red Roofs

1877 / Oil on canvas, 21.5 × 26 in.

Impressionist from the start, Pissarro, who Cézanne called "humble and colossal", was a rigorous artist who used a palette
rich in color. At Pontoise, where he had been settled since 1872, he received and advised Cézanne;
he helped some artists with their first steps, like Gauguin or Mary Cassatt who wrote, "He was such a good teacher
that he could have taught rocks to draw." In the 1880s, he was also one of the first to support
the neo-Impressionists, and even adopted for some time the pointillist brushstrokes of Seurat and Signac.

"...the charm of a simply imaginary limit,
like the scene of a glance embraced
by the framing of the hands".
Stéphane Mallarmé.

ÉDOUARD MANET

On the Beach

1873 / Oil on canvas, 23 × 29 in.

An artist who inspired Impressionists, Manet did not disdain the lessons he received from them, lessons
that allowed him to discover the outdoors. In 1886, Félix Fénéon pertinently described their reciprocal roles,
"The last transformation that turned the tar brusher [reference to his dark colors] of *Bon Bock* into the luminist
of *Linge* and *Père Lathuille* is made under the influence of Camille Pissarro, Degas, Renoir and above
all Claude Monet: these were the leaders of the revolution of which he was the herald."

BERTHE MORISOT

The Cradle

1872 / Oil on canvas, 22 × 18 in.

Student of a painter close to Corot, she met Daumier and Daubigny at the end of their lives. She was a friend of Manet, who depicted her in *The Balcony* and whose brother she married. Is that enough to gain talent? Present at the Impressionist exhibition of 1876, the critic of *Le Temps*, Paul Mantz, wrote, "There is but a single Impressionist in the whole revolutionary group, it is Mrs. Berthe Morisot. Her painting has all the candor of improvisation." Ten years later, Félix Fénéon added, "Mrs. Berthe Morisot is all elegance: wide technique, clear, alert; she is feminine charm without the insipidness."

ALFRED
SISLEY

**Snow
at Louveciennes**

1878 / Oil on canvas,
24 × 20 in.

Strongly influenced
by Corot, Sisley,
a painter of English origin,
participated very early
in the Impressionist
adventure.
A reserved character,
a little bit solitary,
his personality is found
in the brushstrokes
of his works, often marked
by a certain listlessness
that only intensifies
his poetic charm.
Like a number of his
friends, Sisley became
attached to "variations"
of the same subject
at different times
of the day and year,
attempting, as
Gustave Geffroy
emphasized, to freeze
"a little of the fugitive
beauty of eternal things
in his paintings."

*"He was like a really rare companion,
of absolute abnegation, thinking
of others before thinking of himself...
if he thought of himself."*
Gustave Geffroy.

GUSTAVE CAILLEBOTTE

The Floor Scrapers

1875 / Oil on canvas, 40 × 57 in.

Patron of his Impressionist friends when no one wanted their paintings, Caillebotte presented his *Scrapers* at
the 1876 exhibition. The reception was lukewarm. Zola spoke of "a tidy painting like glass, a bourgeois painting."
Others criticized its banality. Nonetheless, Caillebotte proved his audacity, for the centering of the painting,
for his skillful play with shadows and blinding clarity, for the surprising depiction of a series of gestures
that seem to be carried out by the same character depicted at three moments of his work.

JAMES McNEIL WHISTLER

Arrangement in Black and Grey No. 1: The Artist's Mother

1871 / Oil on canvas, 57 × 64 in.

Born in the United States, the painter divided his time between London and Paris. He was a friend of the Realists, Courbet, Fantin-Latour, and Manet, but his works are not easily classified under a precise movement, because he seems to go through all of them. His art lies in the simplicity of lines, which he owes to his taste for Japanese art, the layout, the affectation, and a peculiar atmosphere, a universe that Mallarmé evoked when he spoke of Whistler "the enchanter of a work of mystery as unattainable as perfection." Model for the painter Elstir, in Marcel Proust's works, Whistler expressed his credo as follows, "A painting must be valued solely on the merits of its arrangement."

EDGAR DEGAS

The Dancing Lesson

1873-1875 / Oil on canvas, 33 × 29.5 in.

Trained at Ingres' school, Degas turned towards Manet's Naturalism then settled down with the Impressionists following the 1874
exhibition. But he never really adhered to their principles. Degas' Impressionism was not the variations of light of a landscape,
but mobility, fleeting impressions, and frozen moments. This art is accompanied by delicate tonalities and skillful
off-center layouts, owed to his taste for Japanese art. In 1874, following a visit by Edmond de Goncourt, the latter reported,
"So far, he is the one man that I have seen who can really catch the soul of this life in an imitation of modern life."

*"It is in dark furnished rooms, in cramped quarters
that these bodies with their rich patinas, these bodies bruised
by relations, childbirth, and illness, are studied in detail
or sketched... The lines of this cruel and astute observer illustrate,
through the difficulty of wildly elliptical foreshortenings,
the mechanics of all movement."*
Félix Fénéon, 1886.

EDGAR DEGAS

The Tub

1886 / Pastel on cardboard, 24 × 33 in.

Degas drew *The Tub* in a series of pastels depicting four successive poses of a young woman in her washtub.
The artist's fascination with movement was equaled only by his audacity in framing: here the model is observed
from a low-angle, almost like an intrusion on her privacy. The painting was presented at the last Impressionist
exhibition in 1886. Describing Degas's qualities as a pastellist and colorist, Octave Mirbeau
remembered "the beauty and force of a gothic statue" that emanated from this bather.

MARY CASSATT

**Young Girl
in the Garden**

circa 1880-1882
Oil on canvas
36 × 25 in.

American, trained
at the Pennsylvania
Academy of Fine Arts,
Cassatt made her artistic
career almost entirely
in France. Friend and
patron of Impressionist
painters, she left
a work of great rigor,
mostly handling intimate
scenes. Edgar Degas,
for whose work she had
a real passion, confided
to her one day,
"I cannot conceive
that a woman draws
so well!" Gaugin, evoking
her work and comparing
it to that of Berthe
Morisot, declared,
"Miss Cassatt has just
as much charm,
but even more strength."
Besides her talent,
Mary Cassatt was
the first ambassador
of Impressionism
in the United States.

*"The veritable revolutionaries of form
appear with Mr. Édouard Manet,
with the Impressionists, Claude Monet,
Renoir, Pissarro, Guillaumin, and others still."*
Émile Zola, 1880.

ARMAND GUILLAUMIN

Still Life: Flowers, Earthenware, Books

1872 / Oil on canvas, 13 × 18 in.

Friend of Pissarro and Cézanne, Guillaumin was a painter whose clear, rich and refined palette was enlivened
beginning at the end of the 1880s, to the point that this veteran of Impressionism—he died in 1927—would already
be a Fauvist figure. As Ambroise Vollard recalls, the Tanguy father, who sold paint, was a defender of "these gentlemen
of the *Ecole*": Guillaumin, Cézanne, Van Gogh, Pissarro, Gaugin, and Vignon, to name a few. "To be of the Ecole"
was the equivalent of this other quality: "to be modern", banish the "quid juice" from his palette and "paint thick".

*"No one makes you think of Pascal like Cézanne...
What both of them expressed has this grandeur that is beyond understanding."*
Apollinaire, 1910.

PAUL CÉZANNE

L'Estaque

circa 1878-1879 / Oil on canvas, 23 × 29 in.

L'Estaque, near Marseille, is where Cézanne took refuge during the war of 1870. Seduced by this village not far from his city of Aix, he often came back to work on the motif. Towards the end of the 1870's, Cézanne progressively broke from Impressionist procedures. He stopped exhibiting with his friends in 1878 and withdrew to the south of France. At L'Estaque, a new conception of space revealed itself that Cézanne expressed through color and the simplification of forms, to the detriment of classical perspective. Misunderstood by his contemporaries, he had to wait for the Salon in the fall of 1907, one year after his death, to have his work re-evaluated.

CLAUDE
MONET

**The Rouen
Cathedral.
The Entrance and
the Saint-Romain
Tower, Full Sunlight.**

1893 / Oil on canvas,
42 × 29 in.

Following the *Haystacks*
and the *Poplars* series,
Claude Monet continues
his research: in the years
1892-1893, he sets up
his easle in front of
the Rouen Cathedral.
Here, he wants
to capture the flickering
variations of light
on the old stone façade.

Preceding pages

JEAN
BÉRAUD

**Madeleine
Among the Pharisees**

1891 / Oil on canvas
(detail), 41 × 52 in.

At the Salon de la *Société
nationale des Beaux-Arts*,
in 1913, Apollinaire
described, "Jean Béraud
and his little canvases
of the philosophical
intentions type."
His *Madeleine*, which
illustrates the Gospel
according to Luke
(VII, 36-50), caused
a scandal. Christ, in the
guise of the socialist
journalist Duc-Quency,
confesses his sins to
Madeleine "because
she has much loved,"
where Madeleine would
be Liane de Pougy,
a very prominent
demi-mondaine.
On the left, standing,
sporting a long moustache,
is the painter himself.
In front of him is,
perhaps, Clemenceau.
The philosopher
Ernest Renan is seated,
holding a napkin.
Also present, Alexandre
Dumas, Antonin Proust,
great friend of the
Impressionists, and the
physicist Chevreul whose
work on the simultaneous
contrast of colors
was decisive in the
comprehension of
chromatic phenomena,
especially in
neo-Impressionist work.

After the surrender of 1870, and the repression that followed the Commune, France slowly rebuilt itself on new institutional foundations. In 1879, with the election of Jules Grévy as president, it discovered the virtues of the secular democratic and parliamentary republic—that same year, *La Marseillaise* became the national anthem. Democratic expression widened, sometimes in a conflicting context like the Dreyfus Affair, during the last decade of the century, or the law on the separation of Church and State in 1905. But along with the fortunes and misfortunes of the Republic, a climate of high tension cast a shadow over Europe. Despite the pacifist campaigns that took place in several countries, Jean Jaurès was assassinated in July 1914, and war was declared.

The economic expansion policy of the new regime continued down the road previously followed. Artistic domains followed the same continuity. On the one hand, under the iron rule of political figures that debuted under Napoleon III, the official arts of the Empire were never as well supported as they then were by the Republic. On the other hand, movements that had started under the Empire established themselves. Impressionism was naturally one of these, but also Symbolism. Between these paths, new trails were blazed, that had been unforeseen by the first doctrinaires, like the Naturalism of the 1880s, that combined different styles to describe the social world.

The 1889 International Exhibition was, in this sense, exemplary. In the shadow of the Eiffel Tower, built for the event, the "hateful pillar of bolted sheet metal" vilified by Meissonier, Gounod and Maupassant, the palais des Beaux-Arts presented paintings by Gérôme, Cabanel, Bouguereau, Detaille and Léon Bonnat, the jewels of "pompier" painting, next to—or, at least, near—Manet, Monet, Pissarro and Cézanne. The international section, where the Americans Whistler and Sargent could be found, exhibited a great number of Symbolist artists, like the Englishman Burne-Jones, the Swiss Hodler, the Italian Segantini and the German Stuck.

Lost in the 96 acres of the International Exhibition, the Café Volpini showed the canvases of an "Impressionist and synthesist group": "Gauguin, Anquetin, Bernard and some others, paintings hidden by buffets, beer taps, tables, the bodice of Mr. Volpini's cashier and an orchestra of young Muscovites whose music, played in the vast hall, had no relation to these polychromies," as Félix Fénéon remarked. At the Republic's Exhibition, everyone lived together. There was no accursed art!

Long live the Academy!

No accursed art? If there is any today, it is academic art.

Academic art, the successor of Ingres, respectful of William Bouguereau's credo, "Paint what you see and draw accurately," was then in its golden age, before its decline in the 1920s. Tired of war, people then wanted to forget the bygone world. They wanted light, and they fell in love with the Impressionists. Although disparaged, our "pompier" painters responded all the same to the taste of the leaders; the public appreciated the themes they represented and the quality of their paintings. But they followed unchanging paths. Graduates of the School of Fine Arts knew all about ancient civilization, thanks to the vigilance of their teachers at the Institute. Interns for some time in Rome, at the Villa Medici, they then had to obtain the favor of the people and win official commissions during the annual Salon to win the honors of the Institute. But, other than maintaining a style, these masters were highly conscious of the good work and technical discipline it required.

One recalls Bouguereau telling the young Matisse, "You will never know how to draw." Bonnat went even further, "This man is dangerous, he must get out of here." Nevertheless, numerous testimonies show how much the students respected their professors. Gleyre, who died in 1874, the year of the first Impressionist exhibition, was a fine example. He taught Monet, Renoir and Sisley at his studio; his instruction, as strict as it was, did not stifle the personalities of his students.

So, academic style prospered under the Third Republic, revived by innumerable public commissions meant to renew traditional iconography and praise the Republic of good citizens. The diversity of demand favored the diversity of genres. In a century fond of history, official art tended to reinforce the idea of a secular national identity, and the France of Jules Ferry applauded the representations of Gaulish France in Royer's paintings, or the Merovingian period, as seen in the work of Laurens. Painters of historic, heroic, and military themes, artists like Meissonier, Édouard Detaille, and Alphonse de Neuville, also illustrated the genre, and were echoed by sculptors moved by the same desire for civic education.

More allegory was present, used by decorative painting to magnify science, morals and the arts, in a display of virtuosity, helped by imagery that tended towards subtle sensuality. The viragoes Victory or Knowledge, the ragged beggars, the ingenious orphans, all presented their sculpted nudity, polished and subtly eroticized, "Bouguereautized", exclaimed the Impressionists. This sensualization—which also showed up in Salon paintings, and even religious paintings—could be found in sculpture, feverishly sober in Gérôme's *Tanagra*, or luxuriant in the works of Barrias, who was a master at mixing the most exotic materials.

History, decor, simplified mythology, of course—but society portraits were also important. They could be solemn, when painted by Léon Bonnat, of a "sensual and forced mannerism" with Boldini, or full of the psychological apprehension of the model, which showed aspects of the bourgeois society of the Belle Époque. Portraits, be they standing or head-and-shoulder paintings, also revealed that the boundaries of academic art were relatively indistinct. The unequivocal perception that seems to remain of academic art should not keep us from noticing the existence and permeability of the many channels that it consisted of. Gervex, one of its representatives, a student of Fromentin and Cabanel, and a friend of Bouguereau and Manet, associated with the Impressionists and assimilated their technique and use of light to paint contemporary themes. Zola was right when he wrote in 1879, "Isn't it curious to see how modern inspiration overtakes the best students of academic painters?"

Naturalism or Social Republicanism?

Zola's comment was also appropriate for Naturalist painting. He was the literary champion of this style. So, some painters stemming from Courbet's Realism, followers of artists like Millet, were so humble and attentive, depicting "modern" subjects respecting the fine images of academic art while assimilating Impressionist methods, notably in the treatment of landscapes. They were naturalists like Zola when he spoke of his *Rougon-Macquart* saga as a "natural and social story"—surely, Manet was Naturalist, but not enough to the writer's taste, who judged him perhaps natural but not social enough. Naturalism was also a question of time. This effort to glorify the working world, rural life and honesty, in paintings whose dimensions were more suitable to manifestos than to intimism, could have only arisen from the social Republic, to the point that, beginning in the 1880s, the Naturalism of *The Hayfield* by Bastien-Lepage and Lhermitte's *The Reapers,* became an official art and a movement that touched every European country. This Naturalism was literary and pictorial, yet it also conquered sculpture. When Jules Dalou, who heralded that movement, created his group *Triumph of the Republic,* he did not include a deity of fertility but a real peasant who rolled up his sleeves; the blacksmith is not Vulcan, he is a man at work, driving the chariot of the proud and beautiful Republic that existed only through his effort and will.

"The audacity to invent freely"

To these allegories of reality, to this increasing reality in society (cinematography appeared in 1895), to "the childish method of naturalism", Jean Moréas, in a manifesto published in 1886, opposed Symbolism. It was better to privilege the inner world over the real world, subjective intuition over objective reasoning. In poetry, Symbolism was present in Edgar Allen Poe and Baudelaire before Verlaine and Mallarmé. Beginning already in the 1850s, Symbolism was applied to painting by the English Pre-Raphaelites—Rossetti, Millais, Hunt and Burne-Jones—whose work recalls the primitive Italians. Other precursors were Pierre Puvis de Chavannes and his timeless evocations, Gustave Moreau and his mythological affectation and Arnold Böcklin, who tried to "relate something, give the spectator something to think about like a poem, and leave an impression on him like a piece of music."

The effects of Symbolist thought spread throughout the entire world. Some examples: in Belgium with Fernand Khnopff, in Italy with Pellizza da Volpedo, in the United States with Winslow Homer, in Norway with Edvard Munch, and even in the Baltic region where the painter Mikolaius Ciurlionis was working.

As this movement was open to various influences, it reached all areas of artistic life: music, with Claude Debussy, Gabriel Fauré and Alexandre Scriabine, and sculpture with Medardo Rosso, Rodin and Camille Claudel.

It also proved to be full of promise for the future. Most movements that later blossomed were directly related to it: the Pont-Aven school and the Nabis, the Viennese Secession—with Gustav Klimt, Koloman Moser and Egon Schiele—and Art Nouveau, which irreversibly modified the relationship between all creative styles, whether artistic, architectural or decorative, up to the precursors of the avant-garde.

Marinetti, the "inventor" of Futurism, mentioned the "glorious intellectual fathers: the great symbolist geniuses", while Daniel-Henry Kahnweilerassured that "it is in reading Mallarmé that the Cubist painters will acquire the audacity to invent freely."

77

Painting

FROM ACADEMIC ART to Naturalism, Orsay's intermediate level is dedicated to the arts and decor of the Third Republic, and Salon painting. Also displayed on this floor are the works of the Symbolist movement, except those of its precursors, situated on the ground floor.

ACADEMIC ART and its related styles, with its masters: Cabanel, Gérôme, Benjamin-Constant and Bouguereau, who Apollinaire maliciously called "functionaries of an official art, devoted during their lives to administrative flaws and forgotten by all after their deaths." But he hadn't reckoned with the Orsay Museum.

ACADEMIC ART was on the way out in all genres. Heroic and military painting, for example, was an invention of the 17th century, but in 1870, it illustrated the emotion of defeat. Meissonier, a painter showered with honors under the Empire, painted an epic canvas of the Siege of Paris. Other specialists of military illustrations, like Neuville and Detaille, emphasized the atrocious beauty of the battles. The war also produced some unexpected works in the paintings of artists shocked by the event: Gustave Doré, for example, with his tragic Enigma.

SALON PAINTING with its "uniform paintings like mirrors, in which women can do up their hair," wrote Zola, was dominated by history and mythology in a more or less allegorical style. It was the triumph of Laurens, Bonnat, Cabanel and Lefebvre, present in Gervex's *Jury of Painting*, not to mention Bouguereau, admirer of "celestial creatures, sugared bonbons that melt under the eyes of the beholders." Portraiture also established itself, with Carolus-Duran, who "renders Manet comprehensible to the bourgeois," again according to Zola, and Amaury-Duval and Delaunay, who were succeeded at the end of the century by other portraitists, just as mundane, like Boldini and Blanche. As for decorative painting, virtuous and carefree, it was already present in the former reception halls of the Orsay Station.

THESE ACADEMIC PLEASURES, so esteemed by the elite republicans, were succeeded by the equally valued "Naturalist" collections. Prehistoric Naturalism in Cormon's *Cain*, rustic Naturalism in the works of Lhermite and Bastien-Lepage, whose "superiority over the Impressionist painters is summarized by this: he knows how to achieve his impressions"—once again according to Zola. The works of Jules Breton or Rosa Bonheur renewed the social realism of the years between 1840-1850. Other such artists, who often loved painting canvases with thick paint, include Charles Cottet, and his group known as the Black Gang, in Britain, the German Liebermann, the Russian Seros, the English Walden, who all attest to the European dimension of this movement in the years between 1880-1890.

NEXT TO NATURALISM, or rather opposite it, Symbolism also appeared towards the end of the century; it took shape under the Second Empire with Puvis de Chavannes and Moreau. The great Symbolists were many: Odilon Redon, who seemed sensitive only to the movements of the subconscious, Eugène Carrière, Lévy-Dhurmer and Henri Martin, who combined Symbolism and Impressionism. The international dimension of Symbolist sensitivity is present at the Orsay Museum, with, other than the English Pre-Raphaelites, the most important artists of the movement. These include Degouve de Nuncques, Khnopff with his silence, Arnold Böcklin, Winslow Homer and his ghostly figures, Spilliaert, James Ensor, Prats, Hodler and Baud-Bovy, all painters who embody the words of Jean Moréas, "Dress the Idea in a sensitive form."

LÉON BONNAT

Portrait of Madame Pasca

1874 / Oil on canvas, 88 × 52 in.

Following his passage through Delacroix's studio, Bonnat dedicated himself to religious painting, then became one of the official portraitists of high society during the Third Republic. His art, far from the vivacity of Manet's brushwork, is of an extreme sobriety based on a quasi-photographic representation of his models. Madame Pasca was an actress who debuted in 1864 around the age of thirty.

*"He taught us, with an unprecedented abundance of gaiter studs
and in an unforgettable evocation of patriotic haberdashy,
that the French soldier dreams only of past glories..."*
Octave Mirbeau, 1889.

ÉDOUARD DETAILLE

The Dream

1888 / Oil on canvas, 118 × 154 in.

Student of Meissonier, friend of Alphonse de Neuville, édouard Detaille figures with the latter among
the great military painters of the 19th century. Scrupulous up to the tiniest detail, he possessed a collection
of uniforms and accessories so significant that the Musée de l'Armée purchased it. It is to the Army
that Detaille paid homage to with *The Dream*, where, in a sky washed in tricolor streaks the shadows of heroes,
from Saint Denis to Joan of Arc, up to glories of the Revolution and the Empire, march by.

"When with his children dressed in animal skins,
Wild, livid at the height of the storms,
Cain was made to flee from Jehovah,
As evening fell, the dark man arrived
At the base of a mountain in a great plain..."
Victor Hugo, *The Legend of the Ages*, 1859.

FERNAND-ANNE PIESTRE known as CORMON

Cain

1880 / Oil on canvas, 230 × 275.5 in.

Pupil of Cabanel and Fromentin, history painter and great decorator of the Republic, Cormon specialized in
prehistoric subjects. Here, he illustrates the verses of Victor Hugo dedicated to Cain's flight after the death of Abel.
His care for anatomic representation earned him the name "Father Kneecap" from his students, among who figured
Toulouse-Lautrec, Louis Anquetin, Van Gogh and Émile Bernard. To the latter, he said one day, "You want to do
your black with your blue and your red? I can't keep you with me because you will corrupt your friends."

WILLIAM BOUGUEREAU

The Birth of Venus

1879 / Oil on canvas
119 × 85 in.

Inspired by Raphaël's
Triumph of Galatea,
and giving Venus
the attitude of *The Source*
by Ingres (p. 34),
this work testifies
to the true admiration
that academic artists had
for the Italian master.
Bouguereau himself
bragged of his perfection.
Applauded or deplored,
Bouguereau offers
us here a Venus who is
"probably the most
beautiful example
that we know
of an idealized nude who
at the same time conserves
all of the tactile qualities
of the real world,"
as the American historian
Mark S. Walter
emphasized.

JULES BASTIEN-LEPAGE

The Hayfield

1877 / Oil on canvas, 71 × 77 in.

Student of Cabanel and the Academic school, Bastien-Lepage is one of the artists who,
breaking away from the classical movement, became one of the champions of naturalism in painting.
Zola wrote, "If we study Mr. Bastien-Lepage, we see that he owes quite a bit to the Impressionists;
he took their bright tones, their simplifications and even some of their reflections [...].
It is corrected, subdued Impressionism, made to reach the masses."

GUSTAVE MOREAU

Hesiod and the Muse

1891 / Oil on canvas
23 × 13.5 in.

Influenced by Chassériau, of whose studio he was a regular, Moreau constructed himself a universe where mythological and biblical narratives mingled. In *Hesiod and the Muse*, a gift to the permanent secretary of the *Académie des beaux-arts*, he added a republican lyre placed between the hands of the Greek poet. The peculiarity of Moreau's works, their refinement and preciosity, where richness of details blend with sumptuous colors, were hailed by Symbolist poets, then rediscovered by the Surrealists. This fascination also influenced Victor Segalen, who described the painter in this way, "In the world of words it would be necessary to put the entire array of gem-words out on the tray to describe Gustave Moreau's paintings: green chalcedony and gold beryl, omphax and rubicelle, hyalite and sandastros, solid gold and realgar, onyx, alabaster and this marvelous tyriamethyst, cassidoine eye of the world and cat's eye..."

SIR EDWARD
BURNE-JONES

**The Wheel
of Fortune**

1883 / Oil on canvas
79 × 39 in.

Founded in Great Britain
in 1848,
the Pre-Raphaelite
Brotherhood
was a precursory
movement of Symbolism.
Burne-Jones,
one of its members,
influenced by Italian
painters like Botticelli
and Mantegna,
was also quite affected
by the movement's leader,
Dante Gabriele Rossetti,
painter and poet.
Disdainful of historic
reality, immersed
in literature and
esotericism,
the Pre-Raphaelites
applied themselves
to the representation
of a world of ideals
and purity, a world
fashioned by the humanist
spirit of the Renaissance
expressed by the primitive
Italian painters
who preceded Raphaël.

"His painting, so strange looking and of such deliberate originality,
is painting done for delicate, refined, curious people, those who lived within the
familiarity of the old masters, or whom the boredom of the current art drives
towards the primitives whose childish naiveté awakens their indifference."
Théophile Gautier.

PIERRE PUVIS DE CHAVANNES

Summer

1873 / Oil on canvas, 138 × 200 in.

After studying at the studios of Delacroix and Couture, Puvis de Chavannes seemed to retain the influence
of Chassériau and the Italian fresco painters of the 15th century. His work, which oscillates strangely between
austere Classicism and decorative Symbolism, is based on vast linear compositions carried by chalky bright colors.
From his shadowless beings, fixed in time, from his sober and shallow landscapes, emanate a sensation
of serene eternity to which painters like Gauguin or Maurice Denis were sensitive.

"Each of his paintings incites one to dream...
of the quivering and enigmatic depths of life.
And it is a life without complicated metaphysics...
it is everyone's life, up close, enclosed, concentrated
and full-blown at the same time."
Gustave Geffroy, 1892.

EUGÈNE CARRIÈRE

The Ill Child

1885 / Oil on canvas, 79 × 97 in.

Friend of Rodin and Gaugin, admired by Degas, Carrière completed a work above all intimist and profoundly
humanist; he was one of the founders of the League of Human Rights. Besides portraits of his friends, like Verlaine
and Alphonse Daudet, washed in monochrome browns, Carrière painted themes of childhood and maternity.
This "crepuscular Vélasquez," as Goncourt wrote, painted "children who were looked at by women's faces
with such loving attitudes, like enveloped caresses with profound dark circles around their sunken eyes."

ODILON REDON

Closed Eyes

1890 / Oil on canvas, 17 × 14 in.

In 1888, describing *The Slave* by Michelangelo, Redon noted in his journal, "Behind the closed eyes of his slave there
is such heightened cerebral action! He sleeps, and the worried thoughts that pass behind this marble forehead put ours
in a stirring and thoughtful world." The portrait *Closed Eyes*, which seems to borrow the features of his wife, is no longer
the domain of physiognomic representation; it leads to supernatural intuition, defying all logic, all reason.
In the 1890s Freud was working on interpreting dreams, "a royal path that leads to the subconscious."

WINSLOW HOMER

Summer's Night

1890 / Oil on canvas, 30 × 40 in.

Self-taught American painter, Homer settled at Prout's Neck, in the state of Maine, where he conceived *Summer's Night*.
An enigmatic work, it shows us the sensual presence of two women who dance before nocturnal infinity, unconcerned
about the breaking waves, indifferent to the silhouettes that are but shadows projected onto the sea.
The tension that emanates from the painting recalls that of a verse by Hugo, "Feverish skin, passionate life, electric kiss."
A strange work, it recalls certain Northern European Symbolist artists, Edvard Munch above all.

FERNAND KHNOPFF

Marie Monnom

1887 / Oil on canvas, 19.5 × 20 in.

Trying to define Symbolism, in a text dedicated to Khnopff, Émile Verhaeren wrote, "So the symbol always
purifies itself, through evocation, ideally it is sublime in perceptions and sensations; it is not all demonstrative,
rather suggestive; it ruins all incidentals, all facts, all details; it is the highest and most spiritual expression of art in existence."
Painter of the unspeakable, of the secret, these virtues seem to steal over the traits of Marie Monnom
who was soon to be the wife of another painter: Théo Van Rysselberghe.

Sculpture

AT THE DAWN of the Republic, sculpture became patriotic. Cabet brooded over defeat in *One Thousand Eight Hundred Seventy-one*; Falguière glorified the resistance, The Resistance being precisely the title of the monument built after a snow statue erected by the artist in 1870 on the walls of Paris. In the town squares and on the pediments of public buildings, sculpture demonstrated its pedagogic nature, displaying great men in bronze, marble or stone. Everyone contributed to this educational work, from Aubé and his *Léon Gambetta* to Fremiet, Rude's nephew, who also became the eulogist of national heroes.

ACADEMIC TRADITION supported this Republican sculptural didacticism just as it supported the more "domestic" statuary, oscillating between the allegory and sensuality that Claretie had already described when speaking of the Second Empire, "Carpeaux's girls say: *To pleasure!* Rude's woman cries: *To Arms!*" The decor of the salons was a pretext for the feminine curves of *L'Aurore*, in white and pink Puech marble, and Ségoffin's *Warrior Dance*. In these works, movement hesitated between Baroque giddiness and the voluble twists and turns of Art Nouveau. Sweet and smooth, this repertoire was rich in color. *Nature Revealing Herself to Science*, by Barrias, mixes marble, onyx, granite, malachite and lapis lazuli, in an style where Cordier excelled under the Empire. Even Barrau's *Suzanne* and Gérôme's *Tanagra* were formerly polychromatic. It was Gérôme, king of the "pompiers", who, upon entering the Impressionist room at the 1900 International Exhibition, cried, terror-stricken, "Stop, Mr. President, this is the dishonor of France!" He was in the company of the Chief of State, at that moment.

FRANCE during the 1900 International Exhibition was experiencing the triumph of Neo-Rocaille eclecticism—the Alexandre III Bridge, with its nymphs and water genies, is one of its most beautiful examples. But this taste did not overshadow the emergence of sculptural Naturalism. As in painting, this movement expressed itself through its humility in dealing with familiar scenes: Meunier, with *The Earth*, showed poor wretches succumbing to effort; with Bouchard's *The Docker*, social sculpture extended well into the 20th century. Dalou, Rodin's friend, whether modeling his *Republic* or sculpting the features of Rochefort, was the true herald of Naturalism. But as with painting, the excess of reality led to the backfire of Symbolism, as seen in works by artists like Dampt and Bartholomé. A painter and sculptor, close to Degas, Bartholomé became famous for his funerary art, demonstrating that Symbolist expression is the most appropriate one to convey the unspeakable.

OTHER SYMBOLISTS? Camille Claudel, obviously, and Medardo Rosso, "the prodigious sculptor", according to Apollinaire, whose work is sometimes compared to "Impressionist sculpture". Bartholdi, for example, expressed republican fervor with his *Liberty Enlightening the World*, but the feminine figure that rises above his tomb at the Montparnasse cemetery has Symbolist touches that relate it to Wagner's *Girls of the Rhine* and... Fantin-Latour.

HOWEVER, if there is one name firmly linked to Symbolism, it is Rodin. But is it possible to limit Rodin to just one word? Rodin's energy and power in his Man with a Broken Nose, in 1864, and *The Walking Man*, in 1905, made him one of the key figures in 20th century art, the man for whom "the purest masterpieces are those where you cannot find a single inexpressive scrap of form [...], where everything, absolutely everything can be reduced to the mind and soul."

LOUIS-ERNEST BARRIAS

Nature Revealing Herself to Science

1899 / Polychromatic marble, onyx, lapis-lazuli and malachite
79 × 33.5 × 22 in.

Through the richness and preciosity of the materials used, Barrias, one of the most famous sculptors of the Third Republic, made himself the heir of a virtuous eclecticism that had appeared under the Second Empire. What had changed between the two eras? Splendid anatomies began to reveal their charms. Barrias was also eclectic in his repertoire. For example, he sculpted many busts of personalities, as well as the *Allegoric Monument to the 1870 Defense of Paris*, awarded through a competition in which Bartholdi, Carrier-Belleuse and Rodin also participated, and an alto-relievo that went to the Museum of Natural History in Paris: *The Alligator Hunters* (plaster at Orsay), where the artist hesitated between realism and terror.

JULES
DALOU

The Blacksmith
Preparatory work to
**The Triumph
of the Republic**

1879-1899 / Plaster
26 × 14.5 in.

Student of Carpeaux,
Dalou was exiled
to London for his
participation in the Paris
Commune. A paradoxical
exile since he found
success in Great Britain,
especially for his splendid
intimist statuettes.
Upon his return to France
in 1879, thanks to the
republican amnesty,
he received numerous
official commissions,
one of which was
a high relief for the
National Assembly,
*Mirabeau Responding
to Dreux-Brézé*, and the
immense *Triumph of the
Republic*, whose bronze
weighing over 38 tons
was inaugurated in 1899
at the place de la Nation
in Paris. For Dalou
it was the triumph
of Naturalism in art.

"I always tried to express inner emotions through the mobility of the muscles." Auguste Rodin.

AUGUSTE RODIN

The Walking Man

1905 / Bronze
84 × 63 × 28 in.

Following the failure of *The Man with the Broken Nose* at the 1864 Salon, Rodin returned to sculpture with *The Age of Bronze*. It was exhibited in 1877 and it provoked accusations that he had made plaster models of living models. That same year, he began the modeling of *The Walking Man*, enlarged and cast in 1905. In *L'Art*, published in 1911, Rodin explained his creative process, "Instead of thinking of the different parts of the body as more or less flat surfaces, I represented them to myself as swells of interior volumes. I did my best to convey in each bulge of the torso or limbs the outcrop of a muscle or a bone that developed deep below the skin [...] and so the truth of my figures, instead of being superficial, seemed to blossom from the inside out, like life itself."

MEDARDO ROSSO

**Ecce Puer
Impression
of a Child**

1906 / Bronze
(plaster executed in 1906)
17 × 14.5 × 10.5 in.

Sculptor born in Italy
and naturalized in France
in 1902, Rosso left a body
of work close to the
Impressionist conception
of interaction between
forms and light, work
that seems to abolish
the opposition between
material and psychological
space. "I was struck with
wild admiration," admitted
Rodin, who was influenced
in his own work
by the contribution of
Medardo Rosso.

CAMILLE CLAUDEL

The Age of Maturity

1893-1903 / Bronze
45 × 64 × 28 in.

In 1893, when Rodin
and Camille Claudel
parted company, the latter
began work on what
became *The Age of
Maturity*, the first version
of which was completed
in 1895, the year
of the *Bourgeois de Calais*.
The work displayed
the extent of the drama:
Camille is on her knees,
imploring. Its title is like
a response to Rodin's
The Age of Bronze,
which symbolized
the vitality of youth.

Photography

IN 1883, the Parisian photographer Alphons Liébert wrote, "In the last few years, the gelatin-silver bromide procedure has revolutionized photography, and it could be said that after collodion, which replaced the daguerreotype (in the 1850s), it is the greatest invention ever in the history of our art." Following the glorious years, photography experienced a series of technical upheavals that led its artistic status to be reconsidered.

TECHNIQUE, above all. The works of Richard L. Maddox, and the improvements that followed, aided the development of an argentic emulsion in the 1880s. Photographic art was revolutionized. The faster shutter speeds (1/25 of a second) introduced new techniques and easier to handle cameras. Eastman developed emulsified paper to replace glass plates. During the same decade, optical glass was also improved. But this was not the only mechanical improvement made. A new relationship to photography was introduced, particularly through the birth of an idea full of potential: the snapshot.

JUST AS painting had left the studio for the outdoors, photography could now come out of its studio and discover light and outdoor scenes. Having changed its way of looking at reality because of widespread use, photography won over painters and writers like Degas, Bonnard, Shaw and Strindberg. Even Zola, who indulged in the pleasures of the darkroom, wrote, "You cannot say that you have seen something well if you haven't taken a photograph revealing lots of details that, otherwise, would have gone unnoticed." This was the heart of the creative process of the author of *Ladies' Delight*.

ON THE CONTRARY, photographers sometimes experienced a reality complex vis á vis these other image producers, painters. As soon as photography had been created, in the years 1850-1860, it already tried to assert itself as one of the fine arts. This took place first in Great Britain, thanks to Rejlander, Robinson and Julia Margaret Cameron, pioneers of the Pictorialist movement. This movement, that used soft-focused and dissolved images, and was interested in atmospheric and pictorial studies, appeared in the 1880s in a sort of syncretism of artistic movements. It was a melange of Impressionism, Naturalism and Symbolism, as the work of Peter H. Emerson confirms, sensitive to Whistler and the Barbizon painters.

FOUNDED IN GREAT BRITAIN, Pictorialism was nonetheless an international movement that allowed each artist to express his own personality while establishing a few dominant themes. In France, its two greatest figures were Robert Demachy and Camille Puyo, who used complex tricks to obtain pictorial results or photos with an engraving effect. This can also be found in work by American artists: certain negatives by Clarence White recall the framing of Whistler or the enigmatic universe of Khnopff, whereas Frank Eugene used procedures similar to etching. But like all artistic expression, Pictorialism could not, at times, avoid a certain level of mannerism. More attracted to other forms of expression than to its own style, it always remained, thanks to artists like Alfred Stieglitz and Edward Steichen, open to the future and was able to mix reality and effects.

CLARENCE HUDSON WHITE
The Kiss

1904 / Platinum print, 9.7 × 4.8 in.

Settled in New York in 1906, Clarence White was one of the most representative figures of the American Pictorialist movement. His decorative elegance, his layout drawn from Japanese spirit, visible in *The Kiss*, and his taste for suggesting emotional states, all resemble Symbolist painting. In 1911, regarding his photographs, Joseph Keiley recalled, "the sweet murmur singing of values, with just the slightest trace of the personality that created them."

FRANK
EUGENE
SMITH
known as FRANK
EUGENE

Adam and Eve

1900
Photogravure from
original negative
7 × 5 in.

Born in New York,
Frank Eugene studied
photography in Europe,
then settled in Germany
in 1906. Like most
Pictorialists, Eugene
often turned to the soft-
focus effect but he also
carried out some complex
manipulations, especially
scratching the tips
of negatives before
printing, like in his
Adam and Eve, where
"the figures stand out
against the background
like sensual apparitions
that have difficulty rising
out of the void."
(Ann Hammond)
At that time, the same type
of emotion could be found
in a painting by Carrière,
or in a piece of sculpture
by Rodin or
Medardo Rosso.

Decorative Arts

A CERTAIN permanency of taste extended from the beginning of the Second Empire to the last few years of the century. The phenomenon particularly affected domains where esthetics and functionality combined, like architecture and the decorative arts. This does not mean, however, that no other styles emerged. This is confirmed by the "Grévy style", popular during the first few years of the Third Republic. But it was always the same "official" taste for Eclecticism and abundance that dominated, at least until the reaction to Art Nouveau, in the 1890s, initiated an evolution towards simplified forms.

AT THE ORIGINS of Art Nouveau were several movements. First of all, the English Arts & Crafts movement, which appeared at the end of the 1840s, looking for coherence between architectural design and interior decoration—the idea could be found in France, at that time, when Viollet-le-Duc advocated uniqueness in form and content. The plan won over the Pre-Raphaelites and especially William Morris. In the 1860s, he attempted to unite arts & crafts with industrial distribution.

JAPANESE ART was one of the other major sources of Art Nouveau. Discovered early on at the International Exhibitions, it could already be found in 1866 in a subtle adaptation of a dinner service created by Rousseau and decorated by Félix Braquemond. The Japanese spirit, its lines and framing, also appeared in the works of painters linked to Symbolism, whose suggestions, more than concrete examples, made it one of the driving forces of Art Nouveau.

THIS NEW STYLE was not bound to a single doctrine, yet in all of its expressions, certain recurring principles were apparent: sober forms, quality materials, a reconciliation of the "major" and "minor" arts to create beauty—a "sensual expression of ideas", according to Hegel—that was accessible to all.

LIKE SYMBOLISM, Art Nouveau reached international proportions: Jugendstil in Germany, Secessionstil in Austria, Modern Style in France and Belgium, Liberty in England; its repertoire varied according to school. Geometric in Vienna and Glasgow, most of the centers of creation were inspired by floral motifs. Aspiring to be total art, it extended to architecture and the domestic environment, influencing furniture, ironwork, glassware, jewelry, clothing, posters and book covers.

WHETHER INITIATORS or epigones, many designers imposed this Art Nouveau whose vigor did not subside until World War I. In France, the *École de Nancy* (the Nancy School) was one of the principle instigators, gathered around Émile Gallé and the cabinetmaker-decorator Louis Majorelle. In Paris, Samuel Bing sold exquisite jewelry by Lalique and the sober, wavy furniture of the Belgian designer Henry Van de Velde in his "Art Nouveau" shop, opened in 1895. People like Hankar and Horta worked in Belgium. They imposed the asymmetrical curves of Modern Style on architecture, while Antonio Gaudi offered an exuberant version in Catalonia. Thus, Art Nouveau invaded urban landscapes, from posters by Grasset and Mucha to the voluble arabesque ironworks of Hector Guimard that vibrated on railings and balconies, then drooped in the somber entrances to Paris Metro stations.

RENÉ
LALIQUE

**Pendant necklace
and chain**

circa 1903-1905
Gold, enamel, brilliants
and aquamarines

Jeweler, glass-maker and decorator, Lalique was at the origins of the revival of the art of jewelry, starting from a repertoire of forms characteristic of Art Nouveau: foliated (iris, ivy, anemone) and animal (dragonfly, snake, etc.) decorations associated with the feminine figure. His great originality is owed to the elegance with which he created his jewelry, mixing precious and semi-precious stones (amber, tortoiseshell, ivory) and playing with tonality, iridescence, opacity, and translucency. The jewelry created for Sarah Bernhardt in the 1890s established his reputation; the 1900 International Exhibition assured his international fame.

"The artist does not produce any chemical reaction; he does not reproduce flowers, insects, or landscapes, rather he portrays some characteristic traits, namely the essence of that which has been seen and lived."
Émile Gallé, *Writings for Art*, 1884-1889.

PANNIER-LAHOCHE ET Cie

Vase

circa 1875 / Porcelain, glazed decoration and gold highlights, 10 × 36 in.

The spread of Japanese art is often linked to the name Samuel Bing and his Art Nouveau shop, which opened in 1895. Yet other establishments before his had established a certain reputation in this field. For example, the L'Escalier de Cristal shop, of the Pannier-Lahoche & Cie firm, producer of this vase (belonging to a pair) whose Japanese traits are actually more Chinese than anything else.

ÉMILE GALLÉ

Vase : The Soldanella of the Alps

1892 / Crystal blown and fused at high temperatures, with silver and platinum foils, 44 in, Ø 31 in.

When Gallé returned to Nancy in 1874 to continue the family furniture business, he rapidly became one of the principle revivers of the decorative arts in France. He owed his reputation to the forms proposed, and their decorations (butterflies, orchids, and magnolias) of Japanese inspiration, which relied on incomparable technical mastery: blown glass, cased glass, glass marquetry, metallic and powdered glass foils. Gallé was also known for his ceramics and furniture.

RUPERT CARABIN

Bookcase

1890
Walnut, wrought iron,
and glass
114 × 87.5 × 32.5 in.

This bookcase was
commissioned in 1890
to the cabinetmaker
Rupert Carabin, then
twenty-eight years old
by the industrialist Henry
Montandon. It was paired
with a table with a top
shaped like a closed book,
supported by four
asymmetrically arranged,
nude young women.
The luxuriance of the
foliated decoration
and the interpenetration
of genres, between
furniture and objet d'art,
are poles apart from
the functionality and
elegant curves found
in Henry Van de Velde's
work, yet both are linked
to the Art Nouveau
movement. The same
is found in architecture
where the gracious curves
of Victor Horta contrast
with the exuberance
of Jules Aimé Lavirotte.

HECTOR GUIMARD

Smoking Room Bench

1897
Jarrah, engraved metal
102 × 103 × 26 in.

"Artisan of total art" is how Guimard liked to define himself. Like most Art Nouveau artists, he approached architectural ornamentation with the same tenacity as furniture design and the ironworks of the Paris Metro entrances. His style was based on sinuous curves and the contrasts between open space and empty space. "What must be avoided in all that is continuous, is parallel and symmetry," he affirmed.

HENRY VAN DE VELDE

Desk

1898-1899 / Oak, gilt-bronze and copper
50 × 105.5 x 48 in.

Architect and artisan, like Guimard, Van Velde always advocated functional art, thus rejecting superfluous ornamentation. His work, whose design is based on a principle of coherence between function, form and decoration, is characteristic of Art Nouveau, with its interplay of curves and bends. But the lines have a sobriety and agitation that make it unique.

"The artist will never deplete this abundance
of documentation, this warmth of poetic excitement
needed for decorative composition
and assembled with the help of line and color."
École de Nancy (Nancy School) Program.

ÉMILE
ANDRÉ

EUGÈNE
VALLIN

JACQUES
GRUBER

**Double Door
of the François
Vaxelaire & Cie Shop**

1901
Mahogany, "American"
stained glass, opalescent
glass, gilt-bronze
779.5 × 716.5 × 2.5 in.

Founded in 1901,
the Nancy School included
some of the most
accomplished Art Nouveau
artists. Representative
of the spirit of the
movement, this door,
which came from
a dressing room of a shop
in Nancy, displays
the technical perfection
and confident taste
of the partnership between
three demanding
personalities: Émile André,
architect, Eugène Vallin,
joiner and cabinet-maker,
and Jacques Gruber,
painter and master glass-
maker who worked
for Daum and Majorelle.

*"Of the most sober type, from the simple curve
to the rich details, the decor of contemporary furniture
will have to be very meaningful and reflect life."*
Louis Majorelle, 1925.

LOUIS MAJORELLE

"Orchids" Desk

1903-1905 / Mahogany, letterwood, gilt-bronze, copper, leather, 37.5 × 67 × 27.5 in.

Decorator and cabinetmaker, Majorelle, influenced by Gallé, was one of the most prominent members of the Nancy
School. His furniture, which makes use of mahogany, walnut, maple and Brazilian rosewood, is recognizable
by its elegant curves and proportional lines. It is decorated with gilt-bronze foliated motifs (water lillies, orchids,
seaweed, etc.) of which this desk is a perfect example. Metalwork was also one of Majorelle's specialties; he created
entrance canopies and stair banisters, notably those at La Samaritaine (the famous department store), in Paris.

ALEXANDRE CHARPENTIER

Dining Room at the Adrien Bénard Villa in Champrosay

circa 1900 / Mahogany, oak, poplar, gilt-bronze, 136 × 415 × 244.5 in.

The dining room in the home of banker Adrien Bénard, in Champrosay, is characteristic of a nearly complete
Art Nouveau style arrangement, where woodwork and decorations rely on careful coherence and unity.
The taste for interplaying curves and reverse-curves, as well as the fluidity of forms, can be found there.
Alexandre Charpentier, sculptor, cabinetmaker, engraver, and decorator, entrusted Alexandre Bigot,
a ceramist, with the creation of the fountain and tiles in enameled stoneware.

"Art is a courageous attempt to put life in its rightful place."
Oscar Wilde.

ERNEST
GIMSON

Cabinet

circa 1891
Marquetry of palm,
orange and ebony with
interior in cypress,
sycamore and specks
of silver gilt and metal,
550 × 398 × 178 in.

The historical predecessor
of Art Nouveau, the
Arts & Crafts movement,
appeared at the end
of the 1840s in Great
Britain. Its role was
essential in bringing
art and craftsmanship
together in the United
States and Europe.
It was the first to
encompass all the domains
of the social environment,
from architecture
to interior design
(wallpaper, textiles, kitchen
utensils, furniture, etc.).
Many of its artists,
including Ernest Gimson,
opted for elementary
forms that brought out
the preciosity of the colors
and materials used.

"Establish the right to dare…"
THE PIONEERS OF MODERN ART

Cézanne wrote this
to Émile Bernard, "To deal
with nature through
cylinders, spheres, cones..."
The words are famous.
They summarize this
essential part of Cézanne's
work: the deconstruction
of the pictorial space
inherited from the
Renaissance.
*Apples and Orange*s
constitutes the last stage
where traditional
perspective is abolished.
Cézanne confided in
his friend Gasquet about
his attraction to the silence
of still life, "I've given up
on flowers. They wither
too quickly. Fruit is more
faithful. They love to have
their portrait painted.
They sit there as if asking
forgiveness for having
discolored. Their idea is
given off with their scent.
They come to you in all
their smells, speaking to
you of the fields they've
left behind, the rain that
nourished them, the dawns
that they observed.
Outlining the skin of a
beautiful peach with pulpy
strokes, or the melancholy
of an old apple, I can see
in the reflections that they
exchange the same warm
hint of sacrifice,
the same love for the sun,
the same memory
of dew, a freshness...
There are days when
it seems like the universe
is but one stream, an aerial
river of reflections,
of dancing reflections
around man's ideas."

To Edgar Degas who wanted to write sonnets but complained that he had too many ideas, Mallarmé is said to have responded, "You don't create poems with ideas, you create them with words." During the final years of the 19th century, many other artists also seemed to be concerned by the relationship between the subject to be treated and the artwork to be created. There were many complex reasons for this. Some scientific, like the work on vision and the perception of colors; some sociological, since clientele diversified, and dogmas and mandarins were questioned. Not to mention that in two decades the methods of image production had multiplied, each affirming its own specificity: in the 1880s, photography became "industrialized", the first cinema show took place in 1895, and during these twenty years illustration printing techniques were perfected, the same techniques that are still used today.

This feeling, that pictorial work was not so much a representation of reality as it was a question of technique and material, was not a new one. It could be seen in the works of Delacroix, and was confirmed by Manet. "Our Renaissance began with *Olympia*," said Cézanne. So many stages led to this autonomy from reality, towards the "pure painting" demanded by Apollinaire, towards the disappearance of every external reference, when, in 1910, Kandinsky painted the first nonfigurative watercolor.

1886: The Source of the 20th Century

Chronological markers cannot exemplify the extent of changes taking place; some dates, though, stand out as being important. In 1886, for example, twelve years after the first Impressionist exhibition, the group exhibited together for the last time, having become conscious of the limits of what had been a collective dream. The ties were not broken, but each artist followed his own path, explored his own style. Degas, faithful companion of the Impressionists, experimented with daring framings, unusual lighting, and juxtapositions of tones. Monet, recently settled in Giverny, was overwhelmed by the luxuriance of color, passing through the "magic mirror of reality," as Marcel Proust wrote, to reach the limits of abstraction. Cézanne, who dreamed of making Impressionism "a solid and durable art like museum painting" built himself a universe where color created the space within the frame, where forms were simplified, where foregrounds and backgrounds overlapped, and points of view

were juxtaposed. Braque and Picasso made him their mentor as early as 1907, three years after the death of the master from Aix-en-Provence.

So, they broke up for good at the 1886 exhibition. Not only the Impressionists but also the new generation led by Georges Seurat and Gauguin. Two movements, Neo-Impressionism and Synthesism, called into question this fascination for luminist splendor, and sought to concentrate on more spiritual considerations.

A "polychromatic bunch of minimal dots"

Georges Seurat, initiator of Neo-Impressionism, was noticed at the 1886 exhibition with his *A Sunday Afternoon on the Island of La Grande Jatte.* He based his art on the theories of simultaneous contrast and optical blending of colors elaborated by Chevreul at the end of the 1830s. The mixture of pigments on a palette is aimed at darkening a color, whereas the convergence of colored radiations on the retina, coming from little juxtaposed specks and interacting in a "polychromatic bunch of minimal dots"—according to Félix Fénéon—intensifies chromatic values and models. Sometimes called Pointillism or Divisionism, Neo-Impressionism, which attracted Pissarro for a while, had the advantage of perpetuating a feeling rather than offering "fleeting appearances" of the feeling—again, according to Fénéon—in compositions that showed concern for solidly restructuring volume, whereas Impressionists tended to break them down. Seurat's technique rallied several strong supporters, among whom Henri Edmond Cross, Charles Angrand and Théo Van Rhysselberghe. It also led, thanks to Paul Signac and Vincent Van Gogh—whose style mostly came from Neo-Impressionism—to a true liberation of color, that the Nabis and Fauvists capitalized on.

"I love Brittany: there I find wild and primitive things"

Seurat's suggestions were not trivial. Gauguin's were even less so, guided by the same concerns about the role of color and composition, yet responding to them in different ways. All was within the term Synthesism, which means simplification, or back to basics, not getting bogged down with superfluous lines or tones: we can see here why there was such a fondness for Japanese art, its elliptical style, its framing, its colors distributed in solid areas. A friend of Pissarro, admirer of Cézanne and Degas, Gauguin was also present at the May-June 1886 exhibition with nineteen paintings. He left shortly thereafter for Pont-Aven, in Brittany, where he returned in 1888. "I love Brittany: there I can find wild and primitive things; when I hear the sound of my clogs on this granite ground, I hear the muffled, dull and powerful tone that I look for in painting." This was then popularly called the Pont-Aven school, where a group of young artists gathered around Gauguin, artists like Paul Sérusier and Émile Bernard—the latter initiated him to "cloisonnism", or the delineation of the masses of color of a dark ring to increase their vibration. There is no doubt that this proximity, and the quality of these exchanges, helped Gauguin in return to formalize, if not radicalize his art to attain the pure Idea.

It was also in 1888 that Gauguin met up with Van Gogh in Arles. The latter had abandoned a gloomy Naturalism two years earlier and converted to light through a vibrant and fragmented style. The meeting proved pathetic, and painful. Suffering from repeated hallucinations, interrupted by frequent confinements, this pain that Van Gogh carried inside him, which he expressed through themes of flesh-colored curls and the violence of colors, did not cease until his death, in Auvers on July 29, 1890. Nine months later, Gauguin left for Tahiti "to live in the wild" where he accomplished work immediately recognized by the Nabis, the Fauvists, then by Modigliani and Picasso. All were sensitive to the revelation of "primitivism" in art, worthy heirs to the man who stated, "I wanted to establish the right to dare anything."

The Faith of the Prophets

When Sérusier went to Brittany in 1888, he painted, under the direction of Gauguin, work made up of surfaces of juxtaposed pure colors representing the Amour woods on the Aven. His friends, Vuillard, Bonnard, Denis, Ranson, and Roussel, were struck by its magical nature and entitled it *The Talisman*. Until then, they only had eyes for Gauguin, Cézanne, Degas, the Impressionists and Japanese art. Calling themselves Nabis—from the Hebrew word meaning *prophets*—these young people, joined by other artists like Vallotton, gathered around a credo: "Glorify color, simplify form." Their art, full of mysticism in Denis and Sérusier, totally intimist in Vuillard and Bonnard, sought to rid itself of the hegemony of easel painting, by flaunting decorative ambitions that expressed themselves in various elements of daily life: stained-glass windows, screens, wallpaper, and prints.

Toulouse-Lautrec participated in their first exhibition in 1891. Though he did not share the same point of view as his friends, he demonstrated some concepts that were sometimes close: allusive traits, a tendency towards Japanese-style compositions, but his favorite themes, his sense of foreshortening, and his way of capturing fleeting moments affirmed his originality.

Within the context of "Art Nouveau", "which reigned in the West at the end of the century, the ten years or so of the Nabis adventure left just as visible a trace as the movements that followed, like Gustav Klimt's Viennese Secession. Their common point, whether Nabis or Secessionist was, "To serve total art!"

The Fauvists at the Salon d'automne

Movements, trends, schools—in this end-of-century period the intermingling was such that Émile Verhaeren wrote, "All these trends make me think of swaying kaleidoscopic geometric designs that oppose each other one moment and unite in another, the ones re-enter the others, then separate and flee soon after." If this phenomenon bears a symbolic date, it is 1905, the *Salon d'automne*. There, Douanier Rousseau presented his *Hungry Lion*. His jungle was the *Jardin des Plantes*, his inspiration was academic painting, his charm was poetry. Jawlensky and Kandinsky were also there, and gathered round Matisse were the Fauvists Derain, Vlaminck and Van Dongen. The expression attributed to the art critic Louis Vauxcelles implied that it was no longer a matter of a subtle iridescence of color, "The public was doused with a can of paint," wrote Camille Mauclair. The Fauvists distorted volumes and used strident colors. After a brief encounter that happened by chance between a few young painters, Fauvism had just been founded—at the same time as Expressionism in Germany—when its leading artists already started looking for something new. Braque, who had joined them just a year before, visited Picasso's studio in 1907. There he discovered *Les Demoiselles d'Avignon*. Cubism had been born, the avant-garde was already changing sides. Verhaeren, demonstrating the clash between movements, observed, some time before, that they "still turn in the same circle: new art." On the eve of the war, Apollinaire seemed to echo this thought:

So you are finally weary of this ancient world
Shepherdess O Eiffel Tower the flock of bridges bleats this morning
You've had enough of living in this Greek and Roman antiquity
Here even the automobiles already look ancient

Left

Paul Cézanne seated in front of *The Great Bathers*. Émile Bernard took the photograph in 1904 at the painter's studio in Aix. That year, the *Salon d'automne* dedicated an entire room to his work. The young Matisse also exhibited fourteen paintings there. Louis Vauxcelles wrote, "Without a doubt, the best of the four (Camoin, Manguin, Marquet and Matisse) is Matisse. Today he is very close to Cézanne."

CAMILLE PISSARRO

Portrait of Gauguin

PAUL GAUGUIN

Portrait of Pissarro

circa 1879-1883
Charcoal and pastel
on paper
14 × 19.5 in.

These portraits were probably drawn during one of Gauguin's stays at Pissarro's home. The latter was one of the most ardent defenders of the new generation of artists and even adopted Georges Seurat's Divisionist technique for some time.

Painting

"YOU MUST BE absolutely modern," wrote Rimbaud. This quest for absolute modernity appeared between 1880-1890, guiding the way to the 20th century. The Orsay Museum highlights this adventure in the *Galerie des Hauteurs* where the Impressionists are exhibited, from the early years up to the works accomplished after the dispersal of the group in 1886. On this level the Post-Impressionists are also displayed: the Divisionists, the Pont-Aven school, Gauguin, Van Gogh, Toulouse-Lautrec and the Nabis—the larger paintings of the Nabis are exhibited on the middle level. Finally, on level 4, the Kaganovitch collection is presented, containing an anthology of art in twenty paintings, from Impressionism to Fauvism.

AT THE SOURCE of the 20th century, we can obviously find Monet and Cézanne, both aware of the dead-end into which Impressionism, paralyzed by its passion for light, risked leading them. Monet's *Water Lilies* led us to the threshold of contemporary art, one of lyrical abstraction that present-day artists like Sam Francis and Joan Mitchell claim to use in their work. Cézanne's lyricism was different, enclosed in a new space consisting only of volumes and colors. His *Bathers* and his *Apples and Oranges* were lessons to the Fauvists and Cubists, and participated in the very essence of the art that followed.

NEO-IMPRESSIONISM, and its inventor Georges Seurat, "who should be classified among the greatest" according to Apollinaire, were able to luminously respond to the Impressionist dilemma. Although some masterpieces are no longer in France—*Sunday Afternoon on the Island of La Grande Jatte*, for instance—Orsay contains *The Circus* and *Poseuse de dos*, as well as the major works of his friends. These include Luce and Pissarro, converted Impressionists, as well as Signac, Cross, Lemen, Van Rysselberghe, Dubois-Pillet and Charles Angrand, whom Fénéon said "ingeniously works and manipulates thick plastic paint, configures it in relief, scratches it, scrapes it, guilloches it, and chips it."

BEYOND THE MOVEMENTS, are the "invincibles". Van Gogh, of course, who in just a few months went from bleak realism to harsh light that dazzles Orsay visitors—"Sun, Sun!... Dazzling fault! You who conceal death, Sun..." wrote Paul Valéry. Toulouse-Lautrec, a friend of Van Gogh, mixed lyricism and caricature, stalking movement, like that of the body in *Jane Avril* or *Cha-U-Kao The Clown*, and that of the mind in *The Bed*.

ANOTHER INVINCIBLE was Paul Gauguin, whose career began with well-painted Impressionism and ended in the Tropics, in a continuing quest for immemorial purity, that of *Arearea (Joyousness)* or *White Horse*. His Pont-Aven contemporaries, Émile Bernard, Paul Sérusier and Maurice Denis, so abundantly present at Orsay, understood his message: energy in color, simplification of means. That became the motto of the Fauvists, as well.

EMULATING GAUGUIN, the Nabis also prefigured the artistic adventure of the 20th century. In all of these painters, such as Bonnard and Vuillard, and in all those who joined them, such as Vallotton and Rippl-Ronai, the same taste for delicate colors and audacious framing can be seen. Matisse with *Luxe, calme et volupté*, which oscillates between Divisionism and Fauvism, illustrates an art that was poles apart from the wave of Fauvists, the first artistic revolution of the century. He was joined by Derain, Vlaminck and Braque—the latter, young Fauvist of 1905, two years later created "paintings made up of little cubes", according to the nice words of Henri Matisse.

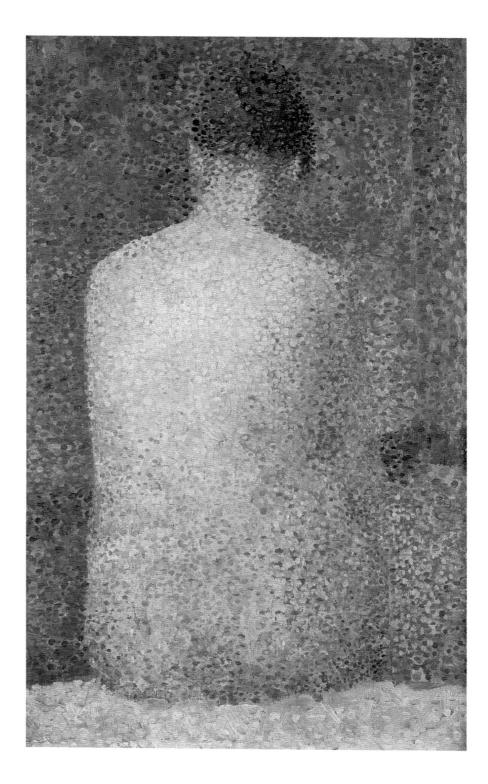

GEORGES SEURAT

Poseuse de dos

1887 / Oil on wood, 96.5 × 61 in.

The Impressionists, other than Pissarro, did not care for Seurat. Renoir joked, "Oh yes! painting with little dots..." The remarkable originality of this painter, who died at the age of 31, was only noticed later.

André Masson praised in him "the supremacy of pictorial imagination over the imitation of poetry," a sentiment common to Surrealism, and André Chastel compared his genius to a "diamond that can only be cut by its own self." The *Poseuse de dos* is one of the sketches for the *Poseuses* of the Barnes Foundation.

CLAUDE MONET

Blue Water Lilies

circa 1916-1919 / Oil on canvas, 79 × 79 in.

After the 1890 "series" in which Monet dedicated himself to capturing, starting from the same motif, the most subtle of atmospheric variations, around 1900 the painter seemed to push his art to extremes: light and color invaded the painting, and swallowed up the eyes.
In a way, the *Water Lilies* ended the Impressionist adventure. In 1927, Paul Claudel noted in his *Journal*, "Thanks to water, which is transparency, iridescence and mirror, Monet made himself the indirect painter of that which we do not see. He addresses this almost invisible and spiritual surface that separates the light from its reflection. The aerial blue captive of the liquid blue."

HENRI-EDMOND CROSS

The Golden Isles

1891-1892 / Oil on canvas, 23 × 21 in.

"Out of respect for a great man, he quickly changed his real name, Delacroix, to Cross," Verhaeren reminded us.
Follower of Divisionism, he went beyond the strictness and scientific constraints of Seurat's art by using his artistic intuition.
Long attracted to the light of the South of France, he joined Signac and Matisse there in the early years of the century.
The "pure and frank tone began to dominate the tints, like a pimento dominates and brings out the taste of food," added Verhaeren.
The vivacity of his strokes and his intensity made him a pioneer of Fauvism.

PAUL SIGNAC

The Red Buoy

1895 / Oil on canvas, 32 × 25.5 in.

Young admirer of Monet, Signac converted nonetheless to Seurat's Divisionism. He was among the best "pointillist" artist to favor
the optic mixture of pure colors by the viewer instead of the painter mixing the colors himself on his palette.
At the beginning of the 1890's, Signac settled in the port of Saint-Tropez where he completed a great number of paintings,
including *The Red Buoy*. The harmonious tones become increasingly vivid under the Mediterranean light, while his
"strokes are proportional to the size of the canvas." It was following Signac that Matisse turned out to be a young Fauvist.

HENRI
DE TOULOUSE-
LAUTREC

**Cha-U-Kao
The Clowness**

1895
Oil on cardboard
21 × 19 in.

He was a student
of the two true jewels
of academic art, Bonnat
and then Cormon,
in whose studio he kept
company with Van Gogh
and Émile Bernard.
But it was mostly
to Degas that he owed
his taste for transcribing
movements, like
a snapshot, captured
in dubious locales of
Parisian life: dance halls,
cafés, and brothels.
*Cha-U-Kao the
Clowness*—exotic
transliteration
of chahut-chaos
or racket-chaos—whom
Toulouse-Lautrec depicted
on several occasions,
was one of the dancers
at the Moulin Rouge
and the Nouveau Cirque.
The unfastening
of the bustier, the sinuous
wrapping and the
transparency of an untidy
yellow tutu:
the spontaneity
of the gesture is reinforced
by the voyeuristic attitude
of a man reflected
in the mirror.

*"If we take the train
to go to Tarascon or to Rouen,
we take death to go into a star."*
Letter from Vincent to his brother, 1887.

VINCENT VAN GOGH

Starry Night

1888 / Oil on canvas, 26 × 36 in.

In 1880, at twenty-seven, Van Gogh began to study drawing then started learning oil painting. Millet was his favorite.
In 1886, he met up with his brother Théo in Paris where he met Toulouse-Lautrec and Gauguin. In 1887, the year of the Sunflowers, he adopted bright colors and fragmented strokes. In February 1888, Van Gogh settled in Arles and wrote to his friend Émile Bernard, "When am I going to do *Starry Sky*, this painting that I'm always thinking about?" Some time later, he painted a nocturne view of the *Rhone River, Starry Night.* Ill, he painted works that resembled his torment. He committed suicide in 1890, in Auvers, at the home of Doctor Gachet, a friend of Cézanne and Pissarro.

PAUL GAUGUIN

Les Alyscamps

1888 / Oil on canvas
36 × 28.5 in.

Having come to join
Van Gogh, Gauguin
arrived in Arles
on October 28, 1888.
A few days later,
he painted *Les Alyscamps*.
The following month,
in a letter, Gauguin
confided the following
to Émile Bernard,
"Vincent and I seldom
agree about anything,
especially about painting...
He is romantic and
I am rather inclined
towards a primitive state."
They split up in
December. Gauguin went
back to Paris. Nevertheless,
his stay in Arles was a
decisive stage in his art:
the color began to flare up.
"Color being in itself
enigmatic in the sensations
that it gives us, one can
only use it enigmatically
to convey the musical
sensations that come from
it, to its nature, to its
interior, mysterious and
enigmatic force.
Through elaborate
harmony, one creates
the symbol." (Gauguin)

"Everything that is exaggerated in a show covers
it with reality and occupies our eyes to the detriment
of our spirit. You have to simplify a show to get the sense of it..."
Émile Bernard.

ÉMILE BERNARD

Madeleine in the Bois d'Amour

1888 / Oil on canvas, 53 × 64.5 in.

When Émile Bernard arrived in Port-Aven in 1888, he was twenty years old, and Gauguin was forty. From their meeting Synthesism was born, an art that relies on the simplification of forms and the vibration of colors used without any relief. That same year, Émile Bernard painted *Madeleine in the Bois d'Amour*. The Bois d'Amour (Woods of Love) is located near Pont-Aven. Madeleine is the painter's sister, but also the "mystical muse" of the artists grouped around Gauguin. Here she is pensive, her body points in the same direction as the Aven River, the peaceful atmosphere is distressed by the verticality of the trees.

PAUL
SÉRUSIER

**The Talisman.
The Aven at the Bois
d'Amour, Pont-Aven**

1888
Oil on wood
10.5 × 8.5 in.

Sérusier arrived
in Pont-Aven in 1888
and painted *The Talisman*
under the direction
of Gauguin.
The work became
the point of departure
for the Nabis. In 1901,
Maurice Denis recalled
this lesson on painting,
"How do you see this tree?
Gauguin had said
in a corner of the Bois
d'Amour: it is very green!
So put some green,
the most beautiful green
on your palette,
and this shadow,
rather blue? Don't worry
about painting it as blue
as possible."
Maurice Denis added,
"That's how we found
out that all works
of art were a transposition,
a caricature, the passionate
equivalent of a felt
sensation."

MAURICE
DENIS

The Muses

1893
Oil on canvas
66 × 53 in.

We are familiar
with this maxim by
Maurice Denis,
"Remember that a
painting, before
becoming a battle horse,
a nude woman
or some anecdote,
is essentially a surface
covered with colors
in a certain assembled
order." Upon the creation
of the Nabis by Sérusier,
Denis was among
its first members,
as well as its theorist
and historian. His work,
whose orientation became
increasingly marked
by spiritualism,
often depicted unreal
atmospheres, penetrated
by silence.

"And nothing's lost
in this striking economy!"
Léon-Paul Fargue.

FÉLIX VALLOTTON

The Balloon

1899 / Paint with spirits and gouache on cardboard, 19.5 × 24 in.

As a young Swiss artist settled in Paris, Vallotton joined the Nabis in 1892.
He adopted their formulations: simplification of lines and volumes, decorative quest, use of color and solid colors.
This elliptical art, and this treatment through masses that was so distinctive in him, were brought to their ultimate
conciseness in woodcuts, giving the sensation that painting and woodcuts sustain one another.
Jules Renard summed it up with these words, "You have a troubling way of being simple."

EDVARD MUNCH

Summer's Night at Aasgaarstand

1904 / Oil on canvas, 39 × 41 in.

As Impressionism began to appear in northern Europe in 1905, some artists expressed, at the end of the 19th century,
the same feeling of unease, or tragic exacerbation in their works. James Ensor, Van Gogh and Munch were among them.
Edvard Munch, a Norwegian, first influenced by Impressionism, turned towards Van Gogh, Émile Bernard, and Gauguin,
who he met in Paris. His art, profoundly symbolic, called on simplified forms, undulating lines,
and violently contrasting colors to express a pessimistic vision of humanity.

GUSTAV KLIMT

Rose Bushes under the Trees

1905 / Oil on canvas, 43 × 43 in.

Leading artist in the Vienna avant-garde scene, between the years 1890-1900, he created the Vienna Secession in 1897,
an Austrian version of Art Nouveau. Then, in 1905, he was one of the founders of the Wiener Werkstätte
that foreshadowed the Bauhaus. His refined Symbolism, be it in erotic suggestions or landscapes, relied
on audacious colors and "textility". Tireless entertainer, among his students figured Oskar Kokoschka
and Egon Schiele who effected the transition from Symbolism to Expressionism.

PIERRE
BONNARD

**Man
and Woman**

1900
Oil on canvas
45 × 28.5 in.

The Nabis loved to give
themselves nicknames:
Jan Verkade, a very big
man, was the "obese
Nabi", and Bonnard was
given the title of "very
Japanese Nabi". But it
would be impossible
to reduce Bonnard to an
elegant and spiritual
painter who was only
influenced by Japanese art.
At the turn of the century,
he developed in a more
personal way, his favorite
repertoire was composed
of indoor scenes, nudes
or landscapes. Associated
with reassuring intimism,
his work nevertheless
sometimes emitted
an almost stifled anguish.
About *Man and Woman*,
Bernard Noël wrote in
Les Peintres du désir,
"The silence brings out of
each pose the same steam
as the dream: you can feel
the lips of the interior
wound just as well as the
aerial gash that already
separates the present from
the past. Everything is
palpable in the air, even
the retreat of the tasty
knowledge of saliva."

HENRI
ROUSSEAU
known as
LE DOUANIER
ROUSSEAU

Portrait of a Woman

circa 1897
Oil on canvas
78 × 45 in.

"This is painting! That's all there is to see here." These words are attributed to Gauguin who, while visiting the *Salon des indépendants* in 1890, supposedly said this about a self-portrait of Rousseau. It is sort of like the "primitive" who would go into raptures when faced with the "naïve". An artist who cannot be pigeonholed by any of the esthetic criteria or movements that prevailed at the turn of century, he was no less admired for his poetic power by Picasso, Kandinsky, Delaunay, Apollinaire, Cendrars and Alfred Jarry who really discovered him. The Douanier's situation, as customs officer (douanier) at a Paris tollhouse, was all the more paradoxical because, conscious of his pictorial "naïveté", he wanted to compete on his own turf with the academic tradition that was his reference. His *Portrait of a Woman*, for example, relied on a concept close to that of *Portrait of Madame Pasca* by Léon Bonnat (p. 78) or the society paintings of Bouguereau or Cabanel. But, like Pissarro exclaimed before a painting by the Douanier, "emotion makes up for inexperience!"

"The delicacy of the tones is surprising and the colors contrast
deliciously. Familiar and charming art!
There is spirit in place of sublimity."
Guillaume Apollinaire, 1911

ÉDOUARD VUILLARD

Public Gardens: Nannies, Conversation, Red Umbrella

1894 / Distemper on canvas, 83.5 × 31.5 in, 83.5 × 60 in, 83.5 × 31.5 in.

Having spent some time in the hands of "Pompier" painters like Gérôme, Robert-Fleury and Bouguereau, Vuillard was
present during the formation of the Nabis. The words of his friend Bonnard could apply to this reserved character,
"All my life I've floated between intimism and decoration." His intimism is one of bourgeois quiet and comfort,
one of the discreet charm of the outdoors where people talk and a few children play, an intimism composed
of subtle arabesques in halftones of refined color that express slightly unveiled happiness.

"Mr. Derain and Mr. Vlaminck who juxtapose, absolutely at random,
dreadful ochre, red, chrome, blue, violet and orange
mpastos that they want us to believe are landscapes or marine scenes.
I thought I was having a nightmare."
"Le Salut public", October 20, 1905.

MAURICE DE VLAMINCK

Restaurant de la Machine in Bougival

circa 1905 / Oil on canvas, 31.5 × 32 in.

Self-taught, Vlaminck tackled painting in an instinctive manner, influenced by Van Gogh who he discovered in 1901.
In 1905, Matisse urged Vlaminck and Derain, with whom he shared a studio in Chatou, to participate in the *Salon des indépendants* and then the *Salon d'automne*. Immediately called *Fauves* (the word *fauves* means wild cats) their exhibition caused a scandal; President Loubet refused to inaugurate the show. "Painting is a party for him," as Apollinaire wrote, though his palette settled down a little bit after 1907. The discovery of Cézanne, one year earlier, was a revelation for everyone.

ANDRÉ DERAIN

Charing Cross Bridge

circa 1906 / Oil on canvas, 32 × 39 in.

Derain's meeting with Matisse at the Carrière Academy and then with Vlaminck in 1900 determined the Fauvism adventure,
"The colors became like dynamite," he confided later. The influence of the movement was considerable yet short-lived.
In 1907, Derain drifted away from Vlaminck, getting closer to Picasso, Braque, and Apollinaire. He was the most audacious
Fauve and the most lyrical, especially during his stays in London between 1905 and 1906, following in the footsteps of Monet.
But under the influence of Cézanne and through contacts with his young Cubist friends, his style became more rigorous.

GEORGES BRAQUE

L'Estaque Landscape

1906 / Oil on canvas, 20 × 24 in.

Slightly older than twenty, Braque became enthusiastic about the Fauves of 1905, who he joined the following year.
"Since I didn't like Romanticism, this physical painting pleased me," he declared later. But as soon as he converted,
he discovered the first example of cubism in Picasso: *Les Demoiselles d'Avignon*. His work once again changed course.
Apollinaire then wrote, "The softness of a Corot combined with great care for the renewal of plastic forms,
that is what characterizes the art of Georges Braque."

HENRI MATISSE

Luxe, calme et volupté

1904 / Oil on canvas, 38.5 × 46.5 in.

"There everything is order and beauty, Luxe, calme et volupté (Luxury, calm and sensual delight)," wrote Baudelaire
in *L'Invitation au voyage.* The canvas painted in 1904, one year before the Fauvist storm, is an essential one in the work
of Matisse: it constitutes the transition between Neo-Impressionism and the powerful colors that are found in his Fauvist work.
Leader of the movement that asserted chromatic peaks, paradoxically he always sought "balanced, pure and calm art",
making his work closer to that of Clouet, Poussin, even Seurat, in its philosophical implication.

Sculpture

AT THE CROSSROADS of the two centuries, academic tradition and the tutelary shadow of Rodin, whose work seemed to stifle all creative inclination, dominated sculpture. Within this context, what is popularly called the "return to style" moved sculpture towards a sobriety and clarity heralding "art deco", which became widespread during the 1920s. Lisse triumphed again, to the detriment of the "innovative" statuary from sculptors from Carpeaux to Rodin: the lines, made with fingers or a knife, were to statuary what the brushstrokes are to painting, multiplying the fragments of material that light could settle on.

ALTHOUGH THE WORK inspired by Symbolism, and created by Paul-Albert Bartholomé, the author of *Monument to the Dead* in the Père-Lachaise cemetery in Paris, appeared in the 1890s to be one of the first manifestations of a return to more idealized forms, the true instigators of this new orientation were Maillol and Bourdelle, both born in 1861.

A TRAINED PAINTER, Aristide Maillol joined the Nabis at the beginning of the 1890s; he turned towards sculpture towards the middle of the decade. In 1905, during the *Salon d'automne*—the Fauvist Salon!—, his plaster of *La Méditerranée* was discovered. In the *Gazette des beaux-arts*, André Gide mentioned the "simple beauty of planes and lines [...]. This is of an impressive weight: the massiveness, the gravity of the head on the arms, the imposing massiveness of the head on the shoulders." Gide also compared the clean, calm work of Maillol to that "uneasy, meaningful work, full of pathetic clamor" by Rodin—also present at the Salon.

BOURDELLE'S HANDICAP was the fact that he was Rodin's disciple. He had the courage to break away from him. A powerful style, intentionally full of archaism, made him great. André Suarès rightfully called Bourdelle an "architect above all". He had the perception of volume and monumentality that also allowed him to find the right continuity between structures and decor during the creation of the bas-reliefs of the Champs-Élysées Theater inaugurated in 1913.

IN THIS EFFORT TO OFFER new methods to sculpture, we cannot forget the work of Joseph Bernard, son of a stone-cutter, and one of the principle architects of the return to the direct cut—many artists still used assistants in their studios. Bourdelle was Rodin's assistant, Rodin had been Carrier-Belleuse's. Another modest hero of the renovation of sculpture, Pompon created a work entirely dedicated to animal statuary. Just like Bernard and Maillol, he loved polished materials; he went straight to the essential.

FAR FROM these esthetic concerns, Gauguin contributed another direction. His sculpted work was marked by a willingness to thoroughly examine the pictorial experience that sought to combine Primitivism and art, the barbarian and the civilized. This activity was a constant concern for him, from *Be Mysterious*, created in Pouldu in 1890, up to the reliefs of his *Maison du Jouir (House of Pleasure)*, in Atuana where he spent his last days. The work of an artist and not a school, it had profound repercussions on the generations to come: when in 1906, three years after his death, the *Salon d'automne* organized a retrospective in his honor, the public discovered twelve sculptures and fourteen pieces of pottery in addition to his paintings. There is no doubt that the fascination that African art exercised on Matisse, Derain and Picasso, and its assimilation into the work of the Fauvists and Cubists, was a result of the primitivism of Gauguin, for whom "the work of a man, is the appreciation of the man."

ÉMILE-ANTOINE BOURDELLE
Penelope

1907-1926 / Bronze
23.5 × 8.5 × 7 in.

In an archaic style, Bourdelle resumed with statuary that was both massive and lyrical. He "tries to give style to the fragmentary art of Rodin," wrote Apollinaire. Simplifying forms, using anatomic deformations to reinforce the expressiveness, he tried to defy a certain naturalism in representations. In 1911, Apollinaire added about *Penelope*, "It is both the statue of Hope and Despair, 'Fair Phyllis, we despair, though we always hope'."

*"I've gotten to work lately, and I labored to produce
a sculpted wood, the matching piece of the first,
'Be Mysterious', of which I am happy,
I even think that I've never done anything similar."*
Gauguin to Émile Bernard, 1890.

PAUL GAUGUIN

Be Mysterious

1890 / Bas-relief, polychromatic limewood, 29 × 37.5 in.

Inspired by his painting *In the Waves*, painted one year earlier, and following another sculpted version,
this polychromatic wood was completed in Pouldu. It seemed to anticipate the "Primitivist" works of the Tahitian era,
this Primitivism that made him exclaim, "Always keep Persian, Cambodian, and a bit of Egyptian in front of you.
The big mistake is Greek, as beautiful it may be." The clumsy carving of *Be Mysterious* and its brutal polychromy,
caught the attention of Maillol, who seemed to remember it in his painting entitled *The Wave*, painted in 1898.

ARISTIDE
MAILLOL

Méditerranée
or **The Thought**

1905-1927
Marble

43 × 46 × 27 in.

Educated in the studios
of Gérôme and Cabanel,
Maillol the painter
slowly gave up the palette
for the chisel.
Of his experience with
the Nabis, he conserved
the simplification of forms,
the rejection of details,
a synthetic conception
of the work that allowed
him to obtain extreme
clarity of composition.
Fascinated by Greek
statuary, he liked to think
of himself as the upholder
of Mediterranean
classicism, applying himself
to generous, fluid and
massive feminine forms.
When André Gide
discovered *Méditerranée*
in 1905, he wrote,
"How lovely is the light
on this shoulder!
How lovely the shadow
where this forehead tilts!
No thought wrinkles it;
no passion torments
these powerful breasts."

FRANÇOIS POMPON

Polar Bear

1918-1929
Lens stone
64 × 35.5 × 99 in.

Assistant to Falguière
and then Rodin, Pompon
first practiced with works
in the Realist style.

He turned towards animal
sculpture in 1905,
dedicating all his attention
to it from that moment on.
He pursued familiar
attitudes through great
soberness in the treatment
of volumes and smooth
cutting, almost to
the point of purity.

JOSEPH BERNARD

The Dance

1911-1913
Marble relief (detail)
33,5 × 206,5 in.

Like many of his
contemporaries,
Joseph Bernard belonged
to a generation of artists
who favored simplicity
and clearness in the
reproduction of forms.
Nothing should
obstruct the idea.
In Joseph Bernard's work
this ambition is expressed
in a new relationship
to material: "granite or
marble, he tackles it
himself with all the respect
due to it, taking care
not to uproot it entirely,
to choose it in a country
that is not too different
from his own," wrote
Léandre Vaillat in 1911.

Photography

IN 1886, recalling the "unfocused vs. sharp" argument in photography, a journalist wrote, "As in the good old days of 1830, what we have before us is the war between Classicists and Romantics." This was the peak of the Pictorialist movement, that is, the "Romantics". Some sided with painting, others were able to look towards a more autonomous conception of their art. From this point of view, the collections of some American photographers were exemplary. These included Coburn, Streichen and, most importantly, Alfred Stieglitz, founder of *Camera Work* magazine in 1903, and of the Photo-Secession group, whose gallery "291" led to the fame, not only of the best artists of the darkroom, but also artists like Rodin, Matisse and Picasso. Aware of the specificity of his artistic language, Stieglitz abandoned Pictorialism in 1907, orienting himself towards an authenticity that inaugurated contemporary photography.

PARALLEL to Pictorialism, color photography, perfected by Louis Ducos du Hauron in the 1860s, was introduced. Improved on by the Lumière brothers at the end of the 19th century, the procedure was not put to use until the dawn of the 20th century when it began to spread rapidly. In 1913, their workshop in Monplaisir, in the suburbs of Lyon, produced around six thousand plaques a day. But it was not until half a century later, with the arrival of new emulsions, that color was able to express itself far from any pictorial reference.

A LABORATORY of techniques and expressions that blossomed during the next century, in the last quarter of the 19th century photography also began to achieve mobility, resolving the contradiction between the modernity of an art form and its incapability of showing the world in movement. Rodin stigmatized this contradiction, contrasting the true lie of the artist with the cold rigidity of photos, "It is the artist who is truthful and photography that is deceitful; because in reality time doesn't stop: yet, if the artist can produce the impression of a gesture created in several instances, his work is certainly less conventional than scientific images where time stops abruptly." It is obvious that the first works on decomposition of movement in the 1880s, those of Muybridge, and of Marey, had consequences on the birth of cinematography in the *Salon Indien* of the Paris Grand Café on that famous date: December 28, 1895.

STIMULATED by photography, influenced by studies made by Jules Marey, even painting became interested in movement: it is present in 1911, in Marcel Duchamp's work, with his *Nude Descending a Staircase*, as well as in his Futurist contemporaries—champions of speed—like Boccioni and Giacomo Balla.

BUT THE IDEA of movement was not only dependant on its decomposed representation; it could also rely on other artifices, especially on photographers like Bragaglia and Lartigue, who played with all levels of suspended time, following in the footsteps of Rodin, explaining that "movement is the transition from one attitude to another".

TO REPRESENT mobility in the world also means to demonstrate the reality of the world. At the beginning of the 20th century, photography was caught up between its desire for beauty and its desire for social purpose. While Stieglitz wanted more truthfulness, modernity is also present in the works of Atget, who decided to humbly capture the little workshops and streets of Paris, or in the profoundly humane work of Lewis Hine who defined his art like this, "Very little technique and lots of heart."

ALFRED STIEGLITZ
The City of Ambition
1910 / 27.5 × 10 in.

In 1880, following his studies in Berlin, Stieglitz returned to New York where he became the tireless defender of photography, publishing the magazine *Camera Work* and multiplying exhibitions. Leader of the American Pictorialist movement, he reoriented the movement in the 1910s, directing it towards a less decorative expressiveness, more sensitive to the facades of Fifth Avenue buildings than to studio work. Moved by urban poetry, he explored it through periods of snow, under the rain, and in the fog, as if to express the psychological tension welling up in the big city.

HENRI
RIVIÈRE

**Couple Entering
a Building**

1885-1895 / Print on
matte argentic paper
5 × 3.5 cm.

A personality of the artistic
Paris of the Belle Epoque,
Henri Rivière was
the creator, along
with Georges Salis,
of the shadow theater
located in the Chat Noir
cabaret in Montmartre.
In addition to handling
the decorations and
production, he also took
some photos backstage.
Illustrator, engraver,
lithographer, his love
of Japanese art is present
throughout his work
(off centered framing,
multiple viewpoints,
the quest for the emotion
of the instantaneous).
This approach can also be
found in his photography.

Decorative Arts

IS THERE a before and after modernity in art history? Evidently, this is a futile discussion, like the argument that would consist of radically splitting the Art Nouveau style into different trends with more or less promising futures. Still, two great movements seem to appear here.

ON THE ONE HAND, Art Nouveau fanned out in a repertoire of foliage, blending floral interlaced designs into audacious curves and counter-curves. Many painters were sensitive to this vocabulary of sinuous lines, mostly born of Japanese art, which became widespread, especially in France and Belgium. Vincent Van Gogh, settled in Arles, wrote the following to his brother Théo in 1888, "Here I will live more and more the life of a Japanese painter." Samuel Bing, merchant and great promoter of Japanese art, called on Nabi artists like Bonnard, Vuillard, Vallotton, Maurice Denis and even Toulouse-Lautrec to design stained-glass windows for the American glass blower Louis Comfort Tiffany. But other than the contribution of these great designers, other than the vitality of this Art Nouveau strictly within the domain of the domestic environment, it also experienced excesses; particularly this degenerate lineage called "noodle style" that still prospers today in the touristy imagery of Montmartre.

ON THE OTHER HAND, Art Nouveau also had geometric aspirations calling for the use of forms where an obvious rationality ruled. Henry Van Velde was not wrong in asserting—as Julius Posener recalled—that "the era of decorations based on gimlets, flowers and women was over: the art of the future would be abstract." There we see the prelude to "art deco" style that stood out between the two wars; the foundations can be found here of the Bauhaus, which pushed the combination of form and function to its limits, and whose lessons were capital in the development of contemporary art.

IN THE DECORATIVE ARTS, this taste for bare lines is found in the 1870s in the English artists coming out of the Arts & Crafts movement. Goldwin, for example, and Christopher Dresser—his silverware models were so modern that they look as if they came from the studio of a designer like Philippe Starck. The work of architect and designer Charles Rennie Mackintosh was just as radical, at the epicenter of the Glasgow school. Advocate of linearity and working drawings, his creations, appreciated in the 1890s, became a powerful inspiration for other designers. This pleasure of elegant sobriety is found in Van Velde, when he worked in Brussels or Berlin. The same spirit, though more radical, emanated from the De Stijl movement in the Netherlands, where the designs displayed a Constructivist purity that echoed these comments by Mondrian, "Art will disappear little by little as life becomes more balanced." Sobriety and functionality were present in Chicago as well, in the work of architects like Sullivan and Frank Lloyd Wright, in Darmstadt with Olbrich and Behrens, or in the Viennnese Jugendstil, where decors still hesitated sometimes between bareness and ornamentation. "Even the cerebral convolutions of the Jugendstil style are lost on ornaments," joked Karl Kraus. But bareness triumphed, with such talented designers as Koloman Moser and Josef Hoffmann, the principal animators of the Wiener Werkstätte, and architects like Otto Wagner and, above all, Adolf Loos, a true pioneer of contemporary architecture.

KOLOMAN MOSER

Paradise
(detail: an archangel)

1904
Tempera on paper
Total size of work:
163 x 305 in.

An accomplished artist, Koloman Moser was the fiercest supporter of the Viennese Jugendstil and one of the founders of the Wiener Werstätte (art studios). Involved in all domains where his creative audacity could make itself felt (jewelry, glassworks, decoration and interior design, posters, furniture, etc.) he created some of the most beautiful objects of Art Nouveau. Requested by the architecht Otto Wagner, Koloman Moser also designed some stained-glass windows for the Saint-Léopold church, of the Steinhof Sanatorium, near Vienna, built between 1904 and 1907.

CHARLES-RENNIE MACKINTOSH

Upright Secretary

1904
White lacquered wood, colored glass, leaded steel, silver-plated brass, 48 × 32 × 16.5 in.

Artist in what is called the "Glasgow style", Mackintosh was one of the principle representatives of Art Nouveau in Great Britain. Architect ("He is a purifier in the domain of architecture," said Mies Van der Rohe of him), decorator, designer and painter, he left his mark in numerous productions (decoration, textile, porcelain utensils, furniture) with meticulously rational forms and a constructivist will based on relationships between abstract squares and rectangles. His lesson was essential for all European Art Nouveau artists who preferred the elegance of geometric forms to the curves of the decorative foliage repertoire.

THONET
BROTHERS

Model no. 4
(on the left)

Model no. 51
(on the right)

circa 1888
Bent beech, canework,
35.5 in

Michael Thonet founded
his company in Vienna
in 1849 after having
discovered a procedure
making it possible to bend
and laminate wood.
This was the first attempt
at industrial furniture
making. The design
of Thonet domestic objects
seduced Jugendstil artists
who drew inspiration
from them, among whom
Josef Hoffmann,
Koloman Moser
and Otto Wagner.

JOSEF
HOFFMANN

Reclining Chair

circa 1908
Bent beech, perforated
plywood, varnished
mahogany, brass
43 × 24.5 × 32 cm.

Like Koloman Moser,
Josef Hoffmann was
one of the prominent
figures of the Viennese
Jugendstil.
His activity was just
as protean as his friend's
was: jewelry, textiles,
glassworks, interior
decoration, furniture, etc.
Besides the singularity
of his work, always
of refined lines, he also
perfected a principle
of ornamentation based
on the principle
of interchangeable
geometric elements.

*"Architecture takes into account the entire physical
environment of human life."*
William Morris.

ADOLF LOOS

Leaf Commode

circa 1902 / Maple brass and marble, 29 × 44 × 22 cm.

Kept out of the Viennese Secession, Adolf Loos published *Ornament and Crime* in 1908, a book indicative of his orientation
that caused a definitive falling out with his friends. Architect above all, the Tristan Tzara villa in Paris is owed to him,
his recourse to purely geometric lines, the rejection of ornament and the use of natural materials strongly influenced
the future of architecture. Loos also designed pieces of furniture where his taste for purity and elegance of materials,
as well as his commitment to functionality, showed through once more.

Ground floor

Sculpture

- Central aisle: sculpture 1840-1875, Carpeaux
- **2** Barye
- **4** Daumier

Painting

- **1** Ingres and followers
- **2** Delacroix, Chassériau
- **3** History paintings and portraits 1850-1880
- **4** Daumier
- **5** Chauchard collection
- **6** Millet, Rousseau, Corot
- **7** Courbet
- **11** Puvis de Chavannes
- **12** Gustave Moreau
- **13** Degas before 1870
- **14** Manet before 1870
- **15** Fantin-Latour
- **16** Open-air painting
- **17** Pastels
- **18** Monet, Bazille, Renoir before 1870
- **19** Personnaz collection
- **20** Mollard collection
- **21** Pastels
- **22** Realism
- **23** Orientalism

Decorative arts

9-10 Eclectism, 1850-1880

Architecture and decorative arts

- **24** Scale models and sets
- **25-27 bis** Architecture and furniture, from William Morris to Frank Lloyd Wright (level 2, 3 and 4)

Exhibitions

" Opera " room
room **8**

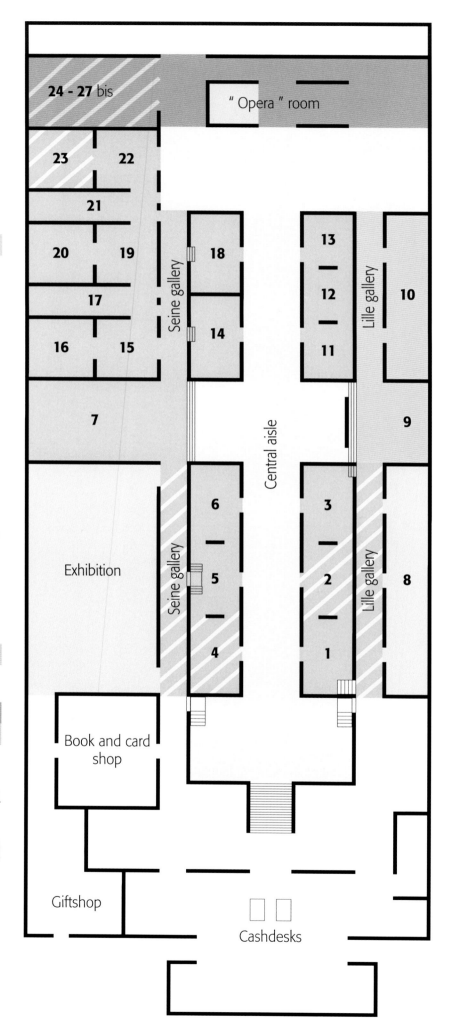

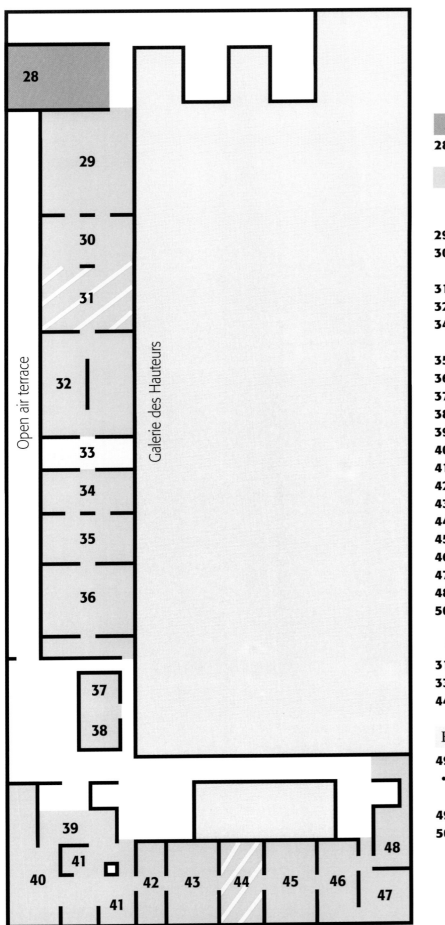

Upper level

Middle level

51 Reception room

Sculpture

52-53 Art and decor
of the 3rd Republic
54 Public monuments
56 Dalou
57 Troubetzkoy
- Seine terrace: Barrias, Coutan,
Fremiet
- Rodin terrace
- Lille terrace: Bourdelle, Maillol,
Pompon, Joseph Bernard

Painting

55 Naturalism
57 Blanche, Boldini, Helleu
58 Naturalism
59 Symbolism
60 Symbolism
62 Redon
70 Denis, Vallotton, Roussel
71 Vuillard
72 Bonnard

Decorative arts

Art nouveau:
61 Belgian furniture, precious objects
62 Ceramics
63 Carabin, Gallé, glassware
64 Guimard, Nancy school
65 North European countries, Dampt
66 Charpentier, Carriès

Exhibitions

Salles **67**, **68** et **69**

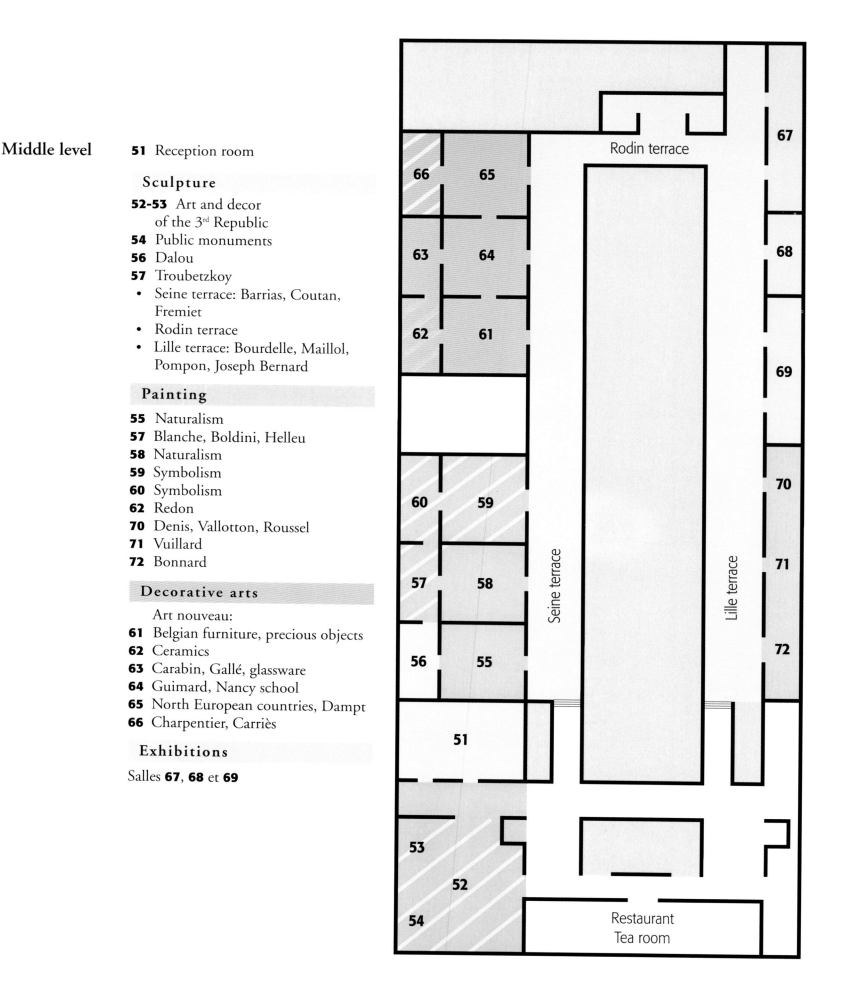

ADDRESS

ORSAY MUSEUM, 62, rue de Lille, 75343 Paris Cedex 07, France. Tel: 33 (0) 1 40 49 48 14

INFORMATION

- Reception desk: 33 (0) 1 40 49 48 48
- Recorded message: 33 (0) 1 45 49 11 11
33 (0) 1 45 49 49 49 (groups only)
- Minitel (French text terminal) 3615 Orsay
3615 Culture
- http://www.musee-orsay.fr

MUSEUM HOURS

- Closed on Mondays
- Tuesday, Wednesday, Friday, Saturday
from 10 a.m. to 6 p.m.
Ticket sales close at 5:30 p.m.
Exhibition rooms begin to close at 5:30 p.m.
- Thursdays from 10 a.m. to 9:45 p.m.
Ticket sales close at 9:15 p.m.
Exhibition rooms begin to close at 9:15 p.m.
- Sundays from 9 a.m. to 6 p.m.
Ticket sales close at 5:30 p.m.
Exhibition rooms begin to close 5:30 p.m.
- from June 20 to September 20, the museum
opens at 9 a.m.

Entrance tickets are valid for the entire day.

Besides its permanent collections, the Orsay Museum organizes a wide array of cultural events like concerts, conferences, lectures, film festivals (auditorium, level 2), as well as educational activities and guided tours.

**ITINERARY
OF THE PERMANENT
COLLECTIONS**

The public can follow a special itinerary of the museum's permanent collection. It is organized chronologically in sweeping sequences of techniques and schools of art.

It covers the three levels of the museum:
- the ground floor first
- then the upper level
- finally, the middle level

N.B. *Exhibitions are subject to change.*
Further information is available at the reception desk.

GUIDED TOURS

"*Discovering the Orsay Museum*" is a basic guided tour available on Tuesdays and Saturdays, in French and other languages. Detailed programs and rates are available at the reception desk.

SPECIAL EXHIBITIONS

Exhibitions, advertised on banners hung throughout the museum itinerary, are dedicated to various themes in a multi-disciplinary spirit. They also include those works that cannot be displayed on a permanent basis at Orsay due to their fragile nature. (Information at the reception desk).

DISABLED VISITORS

Information about the facilities available to disabled visitors can be obtained at the reception desk. Wheelchairs are available at the cloakroom.

RULES AND REGULATIONS

- It is forbidden to take photographs with a flash, smoke inside the museum, eat or drink anywhere beyond the museum restaurant and coffee shop, touch the art work, use portable phones.
- Visitors are not allowed to access the museum with baby carriages or backpack-style baby carriers. Folding strollers are available at the cloakroom.

CLOAKROOM

For the safety of the works of art and the comfort of the general public, visitors are requested to deposit their bags, luggage and umbrellas at the cloakroom (large suitcases cannot be accepted).

BOOKSTORE

The bookstore, card shop and gift shop are open from 9:30 a.m. to 6:30 p.m., and until 9:30 p.m. on Thursdays.

RESTAURANT SERVICE

Access with museum ticket

- Restaurant (middle level)
Lunch from 11:30 a.m. to 2:30 p.m.
Dinner on Thursdays from 7:00 p.m.
to 9:30 p.m.
- Tea room from 3:30 p.m. to 5:40 p.m.
- Café des Hauteurs (upper level):
from 10 a.m. to 5 p.m., on Thursdays
until 9:00 p.m.

Fast Food on the mezzanine: from 11 a.m. to 5 p.m.

BIBLIOGRAPHY

– Pingeot Anne, *Sculpture in the Orsay Museum*, Scala, 1995.

– Rosenblum Robert, *Paintings in the Orsay Museum*, Stewart, Tabori and Chang.

WORKS BY SEVERAL AUTHORS

– Bocquillon-Ferretti Marina, Mettais Valérie and Murat Laure, *A Journey to Orsay*, Réunion des Musées nationaux, 1992.

– *Guide to the Orsay Museum*, Foreword by Françoise Cachin, Réunion des Musées nationaux, 1992.

– Loyrette Henri, Tinterow Gary, *The Origins of Impressionism*, Metropolitan Museum of Art, Abrams, 1994.